5.20.77

CELEBRATIONS FOR TODAY

CELEBRATIONS FOR TODAY

ACTS OF WORSHIP IN MODERN ENGLISH LANGUAGE

STEPHEN W. BURGESS
JAMES D. RIGHTER

ABINGDON   Nashville

CELEBRATIONS FOR TODAY

Copyright © 1977 by Abingdon

Library of Congress Cataloging in Publication Data

Burgess, Stephen W.   1943-
  Celebrations for today.

    1. Liturgies. I. Righter, James D., 1938-   joint
author. II   Title.
BV198.B78   264   76-46429

ISBN 0-687-04804-4

Scripture not otherwise noted is from the Revised
Standard Version of the Bible, copyright 1946, 1952, ©
1971, 1973. Scripture noted TEV is from Today's
English Version of the New Testament. Copyright ©
American Bible Society 1966, 1971. "A Creed for United
Methodists" and "A Creed for People Who Do Not Like
Creeds" by James D. Righter appeared in *God's Action:
Our Affirmation*, published by Graded Press in 1975. "A
Personal Affirmation," "A Christmas Affirmation,"
and "A Creed for Hopeful Skeptics" appeared in *Living
Acts of Worship* published by The Commission on
Worship of the Virginia Annual Conference in 1972.

MANUFACTURED BY THE PARTHENON PRESS AT
NASHVILLE, TENNESSEE, UNITED STATES OF AMERICA

PREFACE

This is an exciting time for contemporary celebration of the gospel of Jesus Christ. People are longing, searching, listening for the Good News as seldom before. Unsatisfied with weekly repetition of bland liturgies, ministers are searching for solid sources of inspiration and are writing their own creative resources. The best of this innovative work is emerging from local churches as pastors plan to lead their local congregations in worship. Here are samples of the work of two such pastors. They are offered to be used as resources for public worship or as starting points for original work others may do.

These acts of worship are celebrative. They strain to share the Good News for our time. That gospel is not just a word of judgment, but also a living word of hope. Worship should sweep people up in love and enjoyment of God, as responses to clear proclamation of God's mighty acts.

These acts of worship are in modern English language. They reflect the way most of us think and talk in America today, rather than repeating historic vernaculars of other times and places. As people speak naturally in worship, they experience acceptance by God and discover who they are in everyday life as people of God.

These acts of worship are specifically biblical and

5

trinitarian. This "conservative" perspective offers the easiest and safest bridge between the oldest traditions of faith and our newest forms of thought and speech. However modern we may feel, we are bound to witness to the gospel whose basic thrusts and limits are set in history and expressed in traditional faith.

ACKNOWLEDGMENTS〜〜〜

The materials in this collection of worship resources are all original, written in the course of pastoral work or for this specific text. Acknowledgment must be given, however, at a number of points.

Where we have paraphrased biblical material, we usually departed from the Revised Standard Version of the Bible. We take full responsibility for departing from that excellent text, at points, to make the language even more forceful.

Where we have quoted directly, we chose the relatively recent *Good News for Modern Man:* Today's English Version of the New Testament.

We must confess that our style of writing and punctuating has been strongly influenced by The New English Bible. It is often necessary to use terse expressions and short sentences, as it does, for public liturgies.

We also thank those lay people for whom we wrote many of the acts of worship and liturgies. Here and there, a creed has grown out of a pastoral conversation; a wedding or funeral service, out of specific settings.

The prayers express longings we have heard in counseling and other settings. Liturgies should flow from the actual life of modern churches.

Our thanks, finally, to our wives and families for the times they have sacrificed to make this text possible.

CONTENTS

CELEBRATIONS FOR TODAY

CALLS TO WORSHIP

1

Out of all our daily times and places, we come to this special time and place to celebrate the Good News of Jesus Christ, together. Let us rejoice and be glad!

2

Praise the Lord! The time has come for us to worship God and to enjoy him together.

3

Seek, and you will find. Ask, and it will be given. Knock, and it will be opened for you. These great promises of Christ call us to long for the goodness of the Lord, for all his blessings to become ours.

4

We gather to praise Jesus our Lord, to confess our sin, to hear his Word in order to live, and to prepare for deeper faith and service. Let us begin now.

5

In the name of the Father, Son, and Holy Spirit, rejoice and be glad. Come with willing hearts and open minds to this time of worship.

6

Welcome to this service of worship. Seek God in Christ, and his Spirit will come. For wherever we proclaim the Word and celebrate the holy sacraments, there is the one true Church.

7

How do we know when God is with us? The sign is this: we shall all be led where we did not plan to go. So we wait for the Word of God to be revealed to us.

8

We could be about a reluctant celebration. If we waited until all was right with the world, we might never come before the Lord God. This is the day the Lord has made; let us rejoice and be glad in it. Then, from rejoicing for no reason, we may discover the strength we need to live.

9

It is amazing! We each come with our individual needs to this very special time and place of worship. We each seek our very own miracle. And the Lord God provides for each and for all of us, as he alone can.

10

Behold the Spirit of the Lord! He anoints us to proclaim Good News, to free all captives, to help the blind see again, and to announce that this is time for all to be accepted by God. So let us rejoice and be glad.

11

Let us turn away from sin and put aside everything that would keep us from worship. Glory in the Lord who made heaven and earth! Thanks be to God! We have the victory through Jesus Christ! All glory and honor, all praise and adoration, all love and thanksgiving be to the Father, Son, and Holy Spirit.

12

The Lord is good in ways beyond believing. If we come to him honestly and openly, he claims us as his own. As we begin our worship, let us long to be filled by the Spirit of Christ.

CALLS TO WORSHIP

13

God's glory is most often revealed when and where we least expect it. In simple faith, let us begin this time of worship looking for those unexpected revelations of the one God whom we call Father, Son, and Holy Spirit.

14

Remember the steadfast love of God. Celebrate the gracious salvation we find in Christ Jesus. Rejoice in the power of the Holy Spirit. This is a time of worship. Prepare to give God glory!

15

God knows each of us intimately and inwardly; let us be ourselves before him. He loves us as a father loves his own. He is saving us through the one Savior of the world. He fills us to overflowing with his Holy Spirit. We can live well, now and forever. What are we waiting for? Let's begin to worship.

16

The most wonderful thing in the world may be about to happen to us. As we seek God, he reaches out toward us to touch our lives and heal us. Give yourself, and receive from God a new selfhood in Christ. As the Holy Spirit fills you, give all you are to this time of worship.

17

Leader: Grace and peace to you and your family this day.

People: And upon the whole household of God, as well.

Leader: May God speak to us as we worship.

People: May he lead us all, as his people.

18

Leader: Come find new life in Jesus Christ.

People: Yes, and joyfully celebrate that new life.

13

Leader: May his love be in each of you.

People: May the Spirit of God be with you, as well.

All: Amen.

   19

In the name of the Father, Son, and Holy Spirit, let us begin. For the Lord God loves for us to worship him.

   20

Leader: What brings you to this place today?

People: We have come as people seeking strength and courage.

Leader: May God be with you in your search.

People: May God be with us all.

   21

Leader: The King of glory is here!

People: Who is this King of glory?

Leader: He is the Lord, strong and mighty.

People: Who is the King of glory?

Leader: He is the Lord of hosts.

People: Praise the Lord God! He is with us!

                              [paraphrased from Psalm 24]

   22

Leader: The earth is the Lord's.

People: Yes. You speak the truth of all ages.

Leader: He has created us as his people.

People: Yes. He has given us life.

Leader: We shall also receive new life.

People: Let us walk in the way of the Lord.

   23

Leader: O Lord, we lift our eyes to you.

People: We trust you, O Lord.

Leader: Teach us your ways.

People: Lead us to your truths.

Leader: All the ways of the Lord reveal steadfast love.

CALLS TO WORSHIP

People: O Lord, lead us in the light of your love forever.

24

Leader: What is the basic purpose of all men and women?

People: Their chief end is to glorify God and to enjoy him forever.

25

Leader: The Lord is the stronghold of my life.

People: He is the light of our homes.

Leader: One thing have I asked of the Lord.

People: One thing do we seek in his house of worship:

Leader: That I may dwell in safety;

People: That we may all live in peace.

[paraphrased from Psalm 27]

26

Leader: I believe that I shall see the goodness of the Lord in the land of the living.

People: Wait for the Lord with courage in your hearts. Yes, be strong and wait for the Lord.

Leader: God is always with us!

People: Hallelujah! Amen!

[paraphrased from Psalm 27]

27

Leader: The Lord is King forever.

People: We worship him as Lord of all.

Leader: May he strengthen his people.

People: May he bless us with his peace.

[paraphrased from Psalm 29]

28

Leader: Sing praises to the Lord!

People: Make a joyful noise to him from the depths of your being.

Leader: Come into his presence with gladness.

People: And bless his holy name.

[paraphrased from Psalm 100]

29

Lord, save your people. Be our God and guide us forever. Amen.

30

Leader: Sing to the Lord a new song!

People: Sing a joyful song of praise!

Leader: Let us sing with thankful hearts.

People: And let us offer him our very lives.

Leader: Our hearts are glad because we trust him.

People: Sing to the Lord a new song!

[inspired by Psalm 33:3]

31

Leader: The Word of the Lord is upright.

People: And he loves righteousness and justice.

Leader: I tell you, the earth is filled with the Word of God.

People: Let all the earth, then, serve the Lord.

Leader: Blessed are all who serve the Lord.

All: Amen.

32

Leader: Who among us desires life?

People: We do! We seek the good life.

Leader: Then live by God's Word.

People: Depart from evil and do good.

Leader: For the Lord looks with favor upon the righteous.

People: Let us seek his peace in serving him.

33

Leader: God is here!

People: We are here!

Leader: Let us begin.

People: Yes, let us worship God.

34

Sing praises to the Lord, and give thanks to his holy name. For the Lord is good, and his mercy endures through every generation.

35

Leader: The Lord directs our lives.

People: He guides us in all his ways.

Leader: In all we do, we are the Lord God's.

People: Praise the Lord! Amen.

36

Leader: Come, let us worship the Lord.

People: Let us give thanks to him.

Leader: He has been good to us.

People: And we are his people.

Leader: The Lord's name be praised!

All: Amen!

37

Leader: The Lord is good.

People: He is very patient with us.

Leader: The Lord leads us.

People: He himself is with us.

Leader: Praise the Lord!

People: The Lord's name be praised!

38

Leader: Make a joyful noise for God.

People: Come, and celebrate his ways.

Leader: He has redeemed us as his people.

People: He leads us, as we serve him.

Leader: Bless the Lord, for his patient love toward us.

People: Bless his holy name.

39

Leader: The Lord is in this place, so let us sing with joy!

People: The Lord is very near; praise and thank him forever!

40

Leader: God is our hope and strength.

People: Thank God he is our companion forever!

Leader: He knows us all too well, yet he will not leave us.

People: Thank God he is our companion forever!

Leader: Thanks be to you, O Lord.

People: Amen. And Amen!

41

Leader: In you, O Lord, I seek refuge.

People: He is a rock, a strong place. He saves us!

Leader: Into your hands, God, we surrender our spirits.

People: We rejoice and celebrate his steadfast love.

Leader: Be gracious unto us, O Lord, in this time of worship.

People: All our times are in his hands, so we are safe!

[paraphrased from Psalm 31]

42

Leader: Come bless the Lord, all servants of the Lord God.

People: We lift up our hearts in the holy place and bless him.

Leader: May the Lord who made heaven and earth bless you.

People: May the Lord who made heaven and earth bless you.

All: Amen. [paraphrased from Psalm 134]

43

Leader: Give thanks to the Lord, for he is good.

People: His steadfast love endures forever.

Leader: Give thanks to the God of gods, to the Lord of lords.

People: His steadfast love endures forever.

Leader: O give thanks to the God of heaven.

People: His steadfast love endures forever.

[paraphrased from Psalm 136]

INVOCATIONS

1

O God, we ask your presence here, now. May Jesus Christ guide all we are and do together. May your Holy Spirit breathe each of us to life. Amen.

2

God, grace this time of worship with your presence and power. Seek out each one of us and minister to our special individual needs. Inspire our fellowship and guide our service of others. Fill us with the mind and Spirit of Christ. Amen.

3

O Holy One, lift us from our own petty business to behold the great future you have for us. Behold the love of God! Behold the miracle of salvation in Jesus! Behold the infilling of the Holy Spirit that we need for worship. Amen.

4

In so many times and ways, O God, you have made yourself and your ways known to others. Reveal yourself to us in this time and place, as we come seeking you. Prepare us for life eternal, in the name of the Father, Son, and Holy Spirit. Amen.

5

Father, you have made us so that our hearts are restless until we seek and find your love. Inspire us by your

Spirit, so that we may discover the mind of Christ, the true will of our Lord, for our lives. To you be the glory, now and forever. Amen.

6

O God of grace, help us to know the joy of the gospel in this time of worship. Inspire our celebration, to make us genuine witnesses to your steadfast love. We worship you because we love you. Amen.

7

Give us grace to be still and know you are God. (*A time of silence.*) Silence the barrage of our words, our thoughts, our feelings. Simply come to us with saving grace. Heal all our inward parts through this worship. Then we shall be able to live as people of God, at last. Amen.

8

O God, Eternal One, claim us as your own. Break into the noise of our worship with the still, small voice that signals your presence. Work the miracle of your love again, for us, here and now. This we pray, in the name of Jesus, by the power of his Spirit in us. Amen.

9

Merciful God, give us in this time of worship the true assurance that we are saved. May peace fill our lives as the love of Christ overflows our souls. Give us yourself, and then we shall be yours in Spirit and in truth. Amen.

10

Creator of our universe, incarnate Son, Spirit of power and peace, live for us as we worship you. Create today a new possibility for us to experience life eternal. Work in these bodies and minds the miracle of salvation. Change what we are and do, according to your will. We long for your presence here, and now. Amen.

11

O God, gather your church in this place. Unite us in the Spirit and the love of Jesus Christ our Lord. Let us hear your saving Word, and go out to do powerful deeds of love and mercy, in your name. Amen.

12

Deliver us from any fear of you, O God. Free us to stand with love and joy in your presence, in this time of worship together. In the name of the Father, Son, and Holy Spirit. Amen.

13

Almighty God, free us from our bondage to sin, so that our whole being may glorify you and enjoy you, now and forever. Amen.

14

Lord God, let all the kingdoms of this world become the Kingdom of Jesus Christ. Begin here and now, to give us your peace and power. We ask that this be a time of good will among people, a time of peace on earth. Amen.

15

Almighty, merciful God, may we continue to grow in grace and in love through your Son, by the power of the Holy Spirit. In time we set aside for worship, prepare us for living now and forever. Amen.

16

O Christ our Lord, who or what can separate us from you? Help us to clear away all that may stand between us and true worship. May we all receive the blessing of salvation and sanctification, starting now. Amen.

17

Eternal God, make all things new, beginning with us. We call upon you in the faith that you do come, and will transform us in faith. Give us the mind of Christ and the power of the Holy Spirit, that we may be refreshed by worship and go on to life eternal. Amen.

18

O God, at the name of Jesus Christ may every knee bend and every mouth confess that Christ is Lord, by the power of the Holy Spirit. We come now into this place to worship and to glorify you as Father, Son, and Holy Spirit. Amen.

19

We long for your presence and power, O God. Be revealed to each of us in our worship together. Amen.

CALLS TO
CONFESSION ~~~~~~~~~~~~~~~

1

Let us be ourselves before God. He knows us inwardly, better than we know ourselves; yet he loves us steadfastly and redemptively. He forgives all, and changes all; so let us confess our sin.

2

What can we confess that God does not already know about us? But confession is good for the soul, and it is healing to receive forgiveness. So let us admit our human weakness before God.

3

Who can stand before the Lord God and not be aware of our personal involvement in sin? We cannot, so as we offer this common prayer of confession, we add to it our own confession of particular sins. Let us be seated, and join in unison prayer.

4

Christ invites us to confess our sin, to receive his forgiveness, and then to go sin no more. Let us now begin that healing, redemptive process by confessing together our human limits.

5

If God were to judge, who could survive? But the Good News is this: if we confess our sin, he is faithful and will forgive us all. Let us therefore confess our sin, and long for the peace of atonement with God.

6

Who can come before God with clean hands and a pure heart? All of us have sinned and fallen short of the glory of God. Come, let us all make our confession.

7

Because of the love of Jesus, we can confess our sin together.

8

God loves us as only a Parent can. Jesus Christ our Lord dared die for us. The Holy Spirit is richly ours. Therefore, as people of triumphant Christian faith, we can confess our sin and seek forgiveness.

9

It is never easy to ask forgiveness. The more we need it, the harder it is to ask. But God provides opportunities like this to meet our most basic spiritual need. Let us offer our prayer of confession.

10

Take a moment to look over the Prayer of Confession in our order for worship today. *(Wait in silence for a time.)* Let us unite our hearts in unison prayer.

11

Let us make our individual, personal prayers of confession in silence today. Then we will offer together our public prayer of confession. Let us pray.

12

It is always easier to see the sins of others than to see our own sin. It is always easier to judge others than to face God's judgment upon ourselves. Now let us make our own inward journey of repentance, as we offer our prayer of confession.

13

How can we flee from God's presence? No matter where we are, or what we do to get away from him and to live on some other basis, he is still with us. In darkness or in daylight, he knows all our ways. Yet he still claims us, loves us, saves us from sin. So let us confess our love for him.

14

Search us, O God; you know our hearts. Put everything we are, as well as all we feel and think, to the test of righteousness, as we confess.

15

Each person should confess his or her sins to God, for this is a time to seek forgiveness. Let us surrender ourselves to a time of genuine confession, in order to receive the forgiveness we need so much. Let us join in prayer.

16

Sometimes we grow weary of confessing our sins. But the Prayer of Confession is there in the weekly ritual, reminding us of our continual need of forgiveness. Let us join, once more, in this very familiar act of repentance. Long for God's grace, as we pray.

17

The Lord God saves all who turn to him. He is our salvation, and our refuge when terror and temptation surround us. Because he has made us, knowing good and evil, we can turn to him for forgiveness. Let us pray.

18

Let us confess our sins to Almighty God. Then we can experience the joy of repentance and the peace that passes understanding. Let us join each other in prayer.

19

We can get angry and unforgiving toward ourselves, unless we have the genuine release of confession and forgiveness. God wants us to confess all we have done, not because he needs it, but because we so desperately require such confession. Now join with me in opening the way for God's forgiving, steadfast love.

20

How can a righteous God forgive? Truly this is the miracle of the Good News that we proclaim. So let us confess our sins.

PRAYERS OF
CONFESSION

1

O Lord, we´ bring you our hearts and minds as reasonable, living gifts. Take us as we are. Our motives are mixed; our thoughts, unclean; and our wills, unfree. Help us to discover what we may become, and guide us to the spiritual power we truly need. We are yours. Mold us into whole persons. Give us peace. Amen.

2

Almighty God, in your presence we confess our human weakness and sin. You have called us to be your people. You have loved us in all our humanity. You remain our steadfast companion in every moment of life. Truly your mercy is beyond our understanding. We trust you enough to make specific confessions: we have wronged you and others in the following ways . . . *(a time for silent confession)*. Forgive us, please forgive us. In the name of Jesus, forgive us. By the power of your Holy Spirit, let us bear fruits worthy of repentance. Amen.

3

We walk the road of faith, each day, in love.
  But we stumble
  And grow weary
  And become impatient.
Our strength is in you, O Lord.
  Heal our disease,

Restore our strength,
And live in us.
Then we will walk the road of faith for others,
And grow in love,
And increase in praise,
And be whole. Amen.

4

Christ, you stir our souls to love you and to follow you wherever you lead us. You fill us with a Spirit that enables us to overcome evil and temptation. What can separate us from God's love in you?

Yet we, each of us and all of us, have chosen and continue to choose to live selfishly. No wonder we fail. No wonder we sin. No wonder we hurt ourselves and others.

Restore us, Jesus, as you claim us again, in love. Heal us in ways beyond our understanding. Give us power to try again. Let our past be past. Show us a new future of meaning and purpose, as we respond to you with all we are. In your name. Amen.

5

Our minds are on one track now, O Lord. We are almost ready to listen. We are almost ready to renew old commitments, and to seek inner renewal. Help us to sort out our motives, and to sweep away the spiritual cobwebs. We need you, to pull it together again. When we are low, love us. When we are tired, give us strength. When we are challenged to start again, give us patience with ourselves. In all ways, give us yourself. Amen.

6

O God, we wonder at your love for us. You know us as we are. You see beneath the surface goodness of our lives. Yet you love us, you save us, you give us eternal life.

We believe; help our unbelief. When we try to do good, evil lies close at hand. Temptations come, as surely as sunrise and sunset. Without your love and your forgiveness, what would become of us? Thank you, dear Father, for your steadfast compassion. Give us the victory in Jesus Christ our Lord. Fill us with the Holy Spirit until nothing can ever be the same again. Amen.

7

On this day, Lord, give me the courage to live one day at a time. I have such high personal ideals; but I sacrifice them just to get by. I think of myself as friendly and outgoing; yet I discover how cross I can be with others close to me. I can define the word "love," but I have so little control over myself in loving others. Lord, one day's faith at a time is enough; not everything about me can be resolved at once. Increase my faith so that I mày take new steps of love. Give me strength for today. Amen.

8

Lord God, our lives confess the miracle of the gospel. But we have been given this treasure in earthen vessels, to remind us that the glory is yours. We know our human sin. We have all fallen short of your glory. But we press on toward the mark of our high calling in Jesus Christ. Send your Spirit to lead us along the Way. Amen.

9

Where do we begin, Lord? To say we are sorry is just not enough. Once we have said it, we still feel empty. Our words are not enough. Lord, how can our feelings reflect our faith? Lord, how can words express our feelings? Lord, how can we come to ourselves, again? Speak to us; your Word heals. Call to us; we are renewed as we respond. We are yours just as we are. Hear us, as we pray now in silence. *(Let there be enough silence for individual prayer.)* Amen.

10

Holy Spirit of God, our human spirits are continually at odds with you. You point us to the Father we would rather not face. You help us see the point of Christ's teachings, when we would rather not understand. You give us power to overcome sin, precisely when we'd rather give in to temptation. Why bother to save us from ourselves? Thanks for interceding for us, when we do not know the Way. Amen.

11

Thank you, Father, for touching us in a special way. We have new love. We are new people. We are filled with joy and peace. We are ready to share your love with others. But we need your help. Live in us. Walk with us so that we will not go astray. This we ask, in Jesus' name. Amen.

12

O God, you have been the refuge of our fathers through many generations. Be our refuge and strength in every time and circumstance of need. Be our guide through all that is dark and doubtful. Be our guard, through all that threatens to undo us. Be our strength in all times of testing. Gladden our hearts with your peace. Amen.

13

We confess, Lord God, that your steadfast love is offered despite all our unloveliness.

We confess, Lord Jesus, that your life, death, and resurrection open for us another way to live.

We confess, Holy Spirit, that your presence and power make all things possible, even our own salvation.

We confess our wonder at being claimed, loved, and saved. In the name of the Father, Son, and Holy Spirit. Amen.

14

O Lord, we come to you to offer our lives, to be part of your Kingdom. We are not always sure of our step; often we cannot plan far ahead. Yet we are yours, Lord. You are a part of us wherever we are. Help us minister to each other and to the world. We want to serve. We want to live. Bring us into larger service, as your people. Come to us, O Lord. Amen.

15

We would be honest with you, O Lord. We are tired, frustrated, nagged by guilt, and unable to change our own lives. So we come to you for strength. Without you, we can do nothing. Without you, we are helpless before our own harmful habits. Now we call on you for the strength you have promised. Heal us where we hurt. Mold us where our lives have been shattered. Fill us where we feel drained of energy. Guide us when we are in danger of missing the way to eternal life. Amen.

16

Almighty and most holy Father, we confess with shame that we have tried to put you off, again and again, with lame excuses. We have been afraid to say no but equally unwilling to respond in faith with an unqualified yes. We are better at debating than we are at acting. Have mercy upon us.

We ask now for your forgiving love, though we do

not deserve it. Do not abandon us to our own fears and weaknesses. Give us the Spirit that sets us free. This we ask in the name of Jesus. Amen.

17

O Lord, hear how our worries and troubles sound. We worry about not having enough time, about having too little money, about what may go wrong, and about what others will think of us. We are captives to our own self-pity; we are often not even concerned about others you give us to love and to serve. Our lives are heavy burdens, Lord.

Is there no easy answer, no ready solution? Are we doomed to worry our way from cradle to grave? Hear, O Lord, and deliver us. Give us the joy and freedom of salvation. As we trust in you, lead us in the way everlasting. Amen.

18

How often have we turned to you, Father? We make confession a habit: an instant replay of our lives, to see where we have been wrong. We do not always approach you with enthusiasm. We have seldom given you our best. We may grow in other areas of life, but fail to grow in faith and in the knowledge and love of Jesus Christ. Fill us with the Spirit that will transform all we are and do. Hear now our silent personal prayers for forgiveness. *(A time of deep silence.)* Amen.

19

Lord God, we pray for this church. Sometimes it disappoints us; we know we must disappoint you. We see the turmoil and the hatred, and wonder: "Where is the Church?" But we are the Church, deeply involved in all the disappointment.

Lord, help us. Show us each the part we have to play

in the building of your Kingdom of heaven. As you direct our lives, we may yet become the Church you need. As you fill us with power, we can serve as the Church in the world. Through your love, we can move into mission. Lord, be with us. Amen.

20

Lord, we are not at all sure why you keep on loving us. We seem to be forever taking half steps, while Jesus runs before us almost out of sight. You have created us strangely, to love you so half-heartedly and so lukewarmly. No wonder you are not satisfied with us as we are. Change us, Lord. Help us find wholeness and direction for our lives. Help us find new openings for friendship and service of others. We do not know what we will be like; except that we know we must grow to be like Jesus Christ our Lord. In his Spirit we pray. Amen.

WORDS OF
ASSURANCE~~~~~~~~~~~~~~~~~~

1

How high are the heavens? Just so great is God's steadfast love for us. How far is East from West? Just so far does he remove all sin from us. As a parent has compassion on children, so the Lord has mercy on all who love him. [paraphrase of Psalm 103:11-13]

2

The Lord is gracious, merciful, slow to anger, patient, kind, a real source of steadfast love. [paraphrase of Psalm 145:8]

3

As we confess our sins, Jesus will forgive our sin and remove all unrighteousness from us. [paraphrase of I John 1:9]

4

God is light. In him is no darkness at all. If we walk in his light, we have fellowship with one another in Christ Jesus, and his Holy Spirit removes all temptation from us. [paraphrase of I John 5, 7]

5

It is hard for us to believe or to understand Christ's great love for us. Yet his meaning is clear: Your sins are forgiven. Go sin no more.

35

6

There is now no condemnation for those who are in Christ Jesus, who walk not by the flesh, but in the Spirit. God proclaims you "Not Guilty." Go live in peace. [paraphrase of Romans 8:1, 4]

7

Ask, and it will be given. Seek, and you will find. Knock, and it will be opened. For all who ask, receive. All who seek, find. And all who knock are welcomed. [paraphrase of Matthew 7:7-8]

8

God so loved the whole world that he gave his only Son. Whoever believes in him shall not perish, but have eternal life. [paraphrase of John 3:16]

9

Let the one who is without sin cast the first stone. For the Lord Jesus gives us the word of grace: "I do not condemn you either. Go sin no more." [paraphrase of John 8:7, 11]

10

Jesus beckons to us: "Come to me, all who labor and are heavily laden, and I will give you peace." May you know the peace of God that comes from knowing your sins are forgiven. [paraphrase of Matthew 11:28]

11

"Let us be convinced together," says the Lord. "Though your sins are like scarlet, they shall be white as snow. Though they are red as crimson, they shall be like wool." [paraphrase of Isaiah 1:18]

12

Give thanks to the Lord of all, for he is good. His steadfast love endures forever. [paraphrase of Jeremiah 33:11]

13

What then shall we say? If God is for us, who can be against us? Who shall bring any charge against God's people? It is God who justifies. Who can condemn? It is Christ Jesus, who died and was raised from the dead, who intercedes for us. I am convinced that nothing in all creation can separate us from the love of God in Christ Jesus. [paraphrase of Romans 8:31, 33, 38-39]

14

I believe that I shall see the goodness of the Lord in the land of the living. Wait for the Lord! Be strong! Take courage! Yes, wait for the Lord. [paraphrase of Psalm 27:13-14]

15

Who is like our God? He pardons sin and forgives transgressions. He does not stay angry forever. He delights in loving us steadfastly. He has compassion on us. He treads all our sin underfoot. He casts all our sin into the depths of the sea. [paraphrase of Micah 7:18-19]

16

Come, let us return to the Lord. He has torn, so he may heal us. He has stricken, so he may bind our wounds. He revives us, and raises us up to live in his presence. Let us therefore press onward, to know the Lord. [paraphrase of Hosea 6:1-2]

17

By God's help, repent and return. Hold fast to love and justice. Continue to wait for your God. [paraphrase of Hosea 12:6]

18

Hear the Word of the Lord: "I will heal their faithlessness. I will love them freely. For my anger has turned from them." [paraphrase of Hosea 14:4]

19

Behold, I create a new heaven and a new earth. The former things shall not be remembered, even for an instant. Be glad! Rejoice forever in what I create! Behold, I create a rejoicing and joyful people. I will rejoice and be joyful in my people. No more shall be heard the sounds of sorrow or cries of distress. [paraphrase of Isaiah 65:17-19]

20

Behold, the time is coming for a new covenant with all people. I will write my law within them, on their hearts. I will be their God. They shall be my people. They shall all know me and love me. I will forgive their unfaithfulness, and I will remember their sin no more. [paraphrase of Jeremiah 31:31, 33-34]

21

May God our Father and the Lord Jesus Christ give you grace and peace. [Philippians 1:2 TEV]

22

Keep on working, with fear and trembling, to complete your salvation, for God is always at work in you to make you willing and able to obey his own purpose. [Philippians 2:12b-13 TEV]

23

We ask God to fill you with the knowledge of his will, with all the wisdom and understanding that his Spirit gives. Then you will be able to live as the Lord wants, and always do what pleases him. Your lives will be fruitful in all kinds of good works, and you will grow in your knowledge of God. [Colossians 1:9b-10 TEV]

OFFERING INVITATIONS, PRAYERS

1

Let us give generously, so we may love the Lord with all our heart, soul, mind, and strength. "For your heart will always be where your riches are." [text from Matthew 6:21 TEV]

2

Let us give all we can, out of love for those the offering will serve. For at the final judgment, "The King will answer back, 'I tell you, indeed, whenever you did this for one of the least important of these brothers of mine, you did it for me!'" [text from Matthew 25:40 TEV]

3

Jesus said to the rich young man, "If you want to be perfect, go and sell all you have and give the money to the poor, and you will have riches in heaven; then come and follow me." As we give what we can, let us offer all we are to Jesus Christ. [text from Matthew 19:21 TEV]

4

When we are wisest, we use our worldly wealth to buy what really matters. "Do not save riches for yourselves here on earth, where moths and rust destroy, and robbers break in and steal. Instead, save riches for yourselves in heaven, where moths and rust cannot destroy, and robbers cannot break in and steal." [text from Matthew 6:19-20 TEV]

5

"If God is for us, who can be against us? He did not even keep back his own Son, but offered him for us all! He gave us his Son—will he not also freely give us all things?" In response to all that God has given and is giving us, let us worship him by offering our gifts. [text from Romans 8:31b-32 TEV]

6

Truly, God is good to us in ways beyond our understanding. Let us offer our gifts to the Lord out of thankful hearts and joyful lives.

7

Out of all that God gives us, what portion shall we return to him? The problem is not that we must justify the offering, but that we must justify what we withhold from God. Come, let us show our love for the Lord in an offering.

8

"The Kingdom of heaven is like a treasure hidden in a field. A man happens to find it, so he covers it up again. He is so happy that he goes and sells everything he has, and then goes back and buys the field." Having found the treasure in Christ Jesus, let us sacrifice what we can to make the prize our own. [text from Matthew 13:44 TEV]

9

"The Kingdom of heaven is like a buyer looking for fine pearls. When he finds one that is unusually fine, he goes and sells everything he has, and buys the pearl." Surely the grace of God is priceless; come, let us give out of thankful, joyful hearts. [text from Matthew 13:45 TEV]

10

"Don't you know that your body is the temple of the Holy Spirit, who lives in you, and was given to you by God? You do not belong to yourselves but to God; he bought you for a price. So use your bodies for God's glory." Make your offering, fully conscious of whose you are. Then your gift will have real meaning and purpose. [text from I Corinthians 6:19-20 TEV]

11

"No servant can be the slave of two masters; he will hate one and love the other." As you give, choose today what or whom you will serve. [text from Luke 16:13*a* TEV]

12

"'You must love the Lord your God with all your heart, with all your soul, with all your strength, and with all your mind'; and, 'You must love your fellowman as yourself.'" Of all that God has given us, let us give what we can out of love for him and for our neighbor. [text from Luke 10:27 TEV]

13

"Who is my neighbor?" we ask. Across the centuries, Jesus reminds us of the Good Samaritan and concludes, "Which of these three, do you think, proved neighbor to the man who fell among robbers?" Let us neighbor someone we may never know, through our gifts today. [text from Luke 10:29*b*, 36]

14

"And Jesus went on to say, 'And so I tell you: make friends for yourselves with worldly wealth, so that when it gives out you will be welcomed in the eternal home. . . . If, then, you have not been faithful in handling worldly wealth, how can you be trusted with true wealth?'" Let us show we can be trusted, by giving God what is rightfully his. [text from Luke 16:9-11 TEV]

15

"'It will be very hard, I tell you, for a rich man to enter the Kingdom of heaven.' . . . When the disciples heard this they were completely amazed. 'Who can be saved, then?' they asked. Jesus looked straight at them and answered, 'This is impossible for men; but for God everything is possible.'" We do not give in order to save ourselves; but knowing we are saved, what can we withhold from God? [text from Matthew 19:23-26 TEV]

16

"You cannot serve both God and money." Let us give part of our money to be used by the Lord God that we serve and love. [text from Luke 16:13b TEV]

17

Lord, accept these personal gifts of love and thanksgiving. Amen.

18

Lord, we give you a portion of what you have entrusted to us. Use what we offer for peace and reconciliation in a world that hurts and hungers for healing. Amen.

19

Here we present this offering to you, O Lord. We also give ourselves as well. Bless us as we give, and move us to serve others, in the name of Jesus Christ. Amen.

20

Bless, O Lord, the giver and the gift. Through what we give, may we find life eternal. Through what we do, many others find Christ as well. Amen.

21

O Lord, you give us every good and acceptable gift to bless us. Now we give to you a portion of what we have, as a sign of our service. Be with us and bless us as your people. Amen.

22

Accept these gifts from our hearts, O Lord. Amen.

23

Here we offer and present, Father, the only gift we have: ourselves. This money is but a symbol of our love and our service. Always remind us of who we are, as we follow Christ. Now may our lives be as acceptable as our gifts. Amen.

24

Father, let this gift represent ourselves, given in service to others, out of the love of Christ, and by the power of the Holy Spirit. Amen.

PRAYERS OF JOYFUL THANKS

1

Almighty God, you have been so creative toward us. You have given us life. You are saving us through Jesus Christ. You fill us with your Holy Spirit, so that our lives overflow with love and grace. How can we ever express our love? Thanks. To you be the glory, now and forever. Amen.

2

How can we ever thank you, Lord? You have given us breath. You are with us in every trial of life. You come to us, again and again, through the Word, Jesus Christ your Son. Words are not enough to thank you. Even serving others is not enough. So we would thank you with every breath, with each new step, and with every deed of mercy. (*Silence, for personal, individual thanksgivings.*) Accept these prayers. Again, thank you, O Lord. Amen.

3

God, you are beyond our wildest imaginations. We cannot conceive the forces creating our universe. We cannot imagine a love so great that Christ died for us. We cannot fully experience the power that is available through your Holy Spirit. You do the incredible in our behalf; so simply, routinely, that we stand in awe of you. We love you. We worship you. We thank you. We look forward to enjoying you forever. Amen.

4

What a wonderful time this is for us, God. And the most wonderful thing of all is that you love us and give us times this joyful and fulfilling. Thank you. Yes, thank you. Amen.

5

We come with thanksgiving in our hearts, O Lord. Our days have sometimes been rough; but we are grateful for time to live. Our church has shown signs of human weakness; yet we are thankful for divine freedom to be your people. Our lives have sometimes been sprinkled with pain; yet we rejoice in the health and personal triumph that you provide. At times we have been anxious; now we thank you for strength and peace. Be with us. And thanks. Amen.

6

You have not set us in a painless, secure, peaceable world. Yet we thank you for making us as we are. We feel at home, even in this kind of world, because you are with us always. Accompany us as we grow in faith and trust in hope for the Kingdom yet to come. Amen.

7

Eternal God, it is so good that you love us. Because of you, all our days are full of wonder and praise. All of life is a great adventure, from cradle to grave. All of life is not long enough to sing your praises. So we look forward to being with you forever. Thank you for such watchful, steadfast care. Amen.

8

How grateful we are, O Lord! We are blessed with freedom to move about with ease. We are blessed with friends with whom we live in peace. You even let us struggle and give us challenges so we may grow. Thank you for the comforts we enjoy. Help us serve in our communities. Truly, your gifts to us are too many to mention. Give us the strength and will to live consistent, thankful lives in the image of Jesus Christ. Amen.

9

Lord, how marvelous it is to feel your presence. How wonderful it is to experience the company of others who also love you. How great it is to discover our lives are being transformed through faith. One of the most moving experiences in life is to worship you. How incredibly fantastic it is to enjoy this life as the beginning of life eternal. Help us start here the things worth finishing in heaven. Again, thank you for all your love. Amen.

10

Father, we enjoy you so much! It is good to worship in your presence. It is exciting to venture each new day, wondering what will be. It is rewarding to see our lives bear fruit, and to see the fruits abide. Let our joy be for ever, in life and in death. Amen.

11

O Lord our God, how good it is to be alive today. Every breath is a reminder that you made us for yourself. Everything that happens seems to sing your praises. Every occasion is an opportunity for love and service. Truly we wish all our times were like this. So we thank you for this day as a chance to celebrate your love. We may not know what our future holds, but we rejoice that your hand holds tomorrow and all our tomorrows. Amen.

12

We remember a time when we did not enjoy life, when our lives were not filled with love, hope, or joy. So we give you thanks, O God. You have made the difference for us between being lost and experiencing our own salvation in Jesus Christ. Thank you for him and for his Spirit that fills our hearts. It is good, not just to be alive, but to enjoy new life as Christians together. Thank you. Amen.

NEW AFFIRMATIONS

1

A PERSONAL AFFIRMATION

I love God the Father with all my heart,
  and with all my soul, and with all my mind.
He works for good, in all things, with those
  who love him.
He is both Creator and creative, a source of
  steadfast love and joy.
To him be praise and honor, glory and might,
  for ever and ever.

I love Jesus the Christ with all my heart,
  and with all my soul, and with all my mind.
He keeps, forever, the souls of all those who
  take up their crosses and follow him.
He is both Savior and saving, a source of
  continual forgiveness and peace.
To him be praise and honor, glory and might,
  for ever and ever.

I love the Holy Spirit with all my heart,
  and with all my soul, and with all my mind.
He makes us sons and daughters of God
  and sets our whole beings free.
The Spirit joins himself to our spirits
  to declare the greatness of God.

To him be praise and honor, glory and might,
   for ever and ever.
I love the One God, who has touched my life as
   Father, Son, and Holy Spirit. Amen.

2

A CREED FOR HOPEFUL SKEPTICS

I wonder who Jesus was, whether he was right about
   how to live in love with others and at peace with
   oneself.
I wonder whether love shall ever overcome hatred, and
   whether one can hate without becoming worse than
   one's enemies.
I wonder whether this life is all there is, or whether it is
   the beginning of something more.
But I am content to live in terms of these concerns,
   without final, proven answers.

I believe that if there is a God who is good, he doesn't
   do half the things for which people blame him.
I believe that this world is the wrong place to look for
   justice, yet one should be loving in dealing with the
   vulnerable and helpless.
I believe in opening oneself to the good and the bad of
   life, in order to be fully human and to find fellowship
   with others who are searching for a way.
But I am content to live on the basis of what I know and
   trust the rest.

I hope that some holy Spirit may change my life, by
   filling it with power, purpose, meaning, confidence,
   and joy.
I hope that suffering and death are ultimate mysteries of

life, for who would want to live in a world where they made sense?

I hope that life, joy, mercy, and peace shall triumph not just in my life, but in all this world.

But I am content to live on the basis of what I hope, which shall not fail me, though life may pass.

I wonder, I believe, I hope, in the name of Whatever or Whoever has touched and healed the lives of so many others. Amen.

3

A CREED FOR ADVENT

Our life flows from the one God and Father of us all:
who created light to fill the dark void of space;
who gave us the light of life to dispel our darkness;
who is the source of light that no darkness can ever overcome.

Our life flows from Jesus the Christ, his only Son, our Lord:
who came into the world, yet the world knew him not;
who was the one true light that enlightens everyone;
who gives, to all who believe, power to become God's own.

Our life flows from the Holy Spirit poured out upon us:
who came with rush of wind and tongues of fire;
who witnessed to all the mighty works of God;
who fills our lives with wonder and purpose.

To our God—Father, Son, and Holy Spirit—be power and wealth,

wisdom and honor, glory and blessing,
now and forever.
Amen.

4

A CONTEMPORARY AFFIRMATION

We worship the Father God, who sent Jesus Christ, to whom the Holy Spirit bears witness.

We worship because we have been called out of our separate lives to be his Church, as a way of saving the whole world.

We worship in the faith that love, joy, and peace shall endure for eternity, as this creative God works his purposes.

We worship, out of grateful hearts, giving thanks and praising this God—Father, Son, and Spirit—who has claimed us.

We worship, acknowledging our sin and our search for meaning, secure in the knowledge that nothing can separate us from God.

We worship, longing for life now and in the future, which is ours for the asking.

We worship, looking for the truth about life and for the right way to live each day.

We worship, listening for the divine Word that comes to us through the Scriptures, the sacraments, the ministries of our fellowship.

We worship, seeking to be a part of God's saving work as we are given the vision and power.

We worship in order that we may be touched and healed by God.

We worship so that our common life may be wondrously changed.

We worship as a preparation for the next chance we shall have to make the difference in someone's life or in some crucial situation.

In the name of all that is Holy: Father, Son, and Spirit. Amen.

5

A CHRISTMAS AFFIRMATION

I believe that Christmas is more than toys, gifts, and sparkling trees. It is the celebration of the birthday of God's very special Son. And I believe that my response to him is a joyous renewal of my life.

I believe that this "Child of Hope" grew to maturity and followed God's will perfectly. My response to him is as simple as listening to God, and as hard as doing what he wants me to do.

I believe that the "Prince of Peace" has a dream for us—one we have not fully lived as his people. My response to him is nothing short of giving that peace to another person.

I believe God sent love to us—not the soft, plastic variety—but a love of courage and strength. My response is a renewal of my energy to serve him.

I believe God gave us joy—the gift of smiles and laughter. He did not intend for me to frown his love, but to share it through smiles.

I believe that as I stand in this season of joy, my life is a changed celebration of his Kingdom of Peace. Amen.

6

A CHRISTIAN AFFIRMATION

I believe in God as Father and Creator of all things that are.

I believe that out of his love for us, he sustains life in sorrow and in joy.

I believe in Jesus Christ, God's Son.

I believe that through his death and resurrection, he opens the doors of faith and shows the meaning of life.

His promises and his love give richness and depth to life.

I believe in the Holy Spirit as the divine spark which drives everyone to seek closer communion with God.

I believe he changes life from discord to harmony and fills our emptiness with the abundance of heaven.

I believe in the sanctity of life, the finality of death, and the hope of the Resurrection.

Thanks be to God! Amen.

7

A JOYFUL PROCLAMATION

God is real! I can feel him and I know he is near.

When I feel lonely and discouraged, I can count on him.

He is close enough to me that I can respond to him.

He calls me to support and to affirm others.

God is love! He sent Jesus to die for me.

I need no other proof of divine compassion.

His constant love for me is strong.
He calls me to be his disciple.

God cares about me! The Holy Spirit fills my life.
His Spirit touches me and turns me to unexpected paths.
A new way opens when I'm against a blind wall.
God is all I need for a creative life!

I belong to God! Our love for each other will last forever.
The best response I can make to him is my total energy.
I will put away all things that separate me from God.
I need God, and enjoy God, now and forever. Amen.

8

AN EXPRESSION OF FAITH

We believe in the gathered community of faith. Through it, we learn to love and to value life. In it, we find acceptance.

We believe in the wholeness of life. We are not intended to be split and divided as persons. We are created and set in a fractured world, so that we can bring it to wholeness as well.

We believe in one God expressed in three ways: Father, Son, and Spirit. When we worship one, we acknowledge all. When we are troubled, God responds according to our needs.

We believe in the flow of life, from birth through death into everlasting life. We cannot capture the wonder of life before God with explanations. We only know God is with us. Thanks be to God!

9

A CREED

We believe in one God—our creator. We owe him our total lives.

We believe in Jesus Christ—our example. We owe him all our energy.

We believe in the Spirit—our comforter. We owe him total enthusiasm.

We believe in the Church—our community. It is not perfect, but we owe it nothing short of total involvement.

We believe in the Word—our Bible. It is a record of God's activity.

We owe God our very lives, to continue the story of salvation. Amen.

10

A RESPONSIVE AFFIRMATION

Minister: What is it that guides me, when all is quiet and hushed?

People: It is the voice of God, invading my private world of thoughts.

Minister: What is it that holds me together, when pressures threaten me?

People: It is knowing that Christ endured life and death. As I am a part of him, I can endure, too!

Minister: Who shares the ups and downs of my daily living?

People: It is the Spirit who comforts and sustains, as I am filled with life eternal.

Minister: How can I respond to these gifts from God?

People: I will give him my energy and my enthusiasm as I serve.

All: Amen.

11

AN UNDERSTANDING OF THE CHURCH

We are the Church! Wherever we live, work, and play—we are the Church!

We are its arms, legs, and feet, but God is the head.

We are the life of the Church—in fellowship, prayer, and personal growth.

We are the love God creates in the Church—for all people.

We are the mission of the Church: available, concerned, and committed.

We are the Church! God is with us!

12

AN UNDERSTANDING OF CHRIST

We believe in the gift of Bethlehem.

His advent was a cattle stall.

His proclamation was a star.

His celebration began with shepherds.

He is meant for us—today.

We believe in the gift of Jerusalem.

His advent was a priestly discussion.

His proclamation was a new mission.

His celebration began on a solemn hill.
He is meant for our maturing faith.

We believe in the gift of Calvary.
His advent was an empty tomb.
His proclamation was a Resurrection.
His celebration is a Kingdom.
He is our hope.

We believe. We live by our beliefs.
Our advent is a gift from God.
Our proclamation is a risen Lord.
Our celebration is a Resurrection.
Our lives are his Kingdom.

Thanks be to God for Jesus Christ! Amen.

13

A CREED FOR PEOPLE WHO DO NOT LIKE CREEDS

I believe the Good News is no system of doctrine;
nor is it a philosophy of the universe.
The Good News simply points us toward God.

No creed is required for me to be a Christian.
I will do, as best I can, the will of God.
He is my Father, and he will always care for me.

Jesus was conscious, in a special way,
of what it means to be a son of God.
I join him in affirming I am a child of God, too.

This attitude, this Spirit, and its fruits in life
are the only test, for me, of right belief
And the only proof of the truth of faith in God.

The good news simply puts the living God before us.
    I believe him; I obey his will.
Faith is simple, because it was meant to be done.

I believe this. Amen.

14
A CREED FOR UNITED METHODISTS
We believe in God our Father,
    who creates the universe and our earth;
    who continues to care for us.

We believe in our Lord Jesus Christ,
    who redeems creation and all people;
    who continues to live in us.

We believe in the Holy Spirit,
    who empowers renewal and ministry;
    who continues to work through us.

We believe that Scripture, tradition,
    experience, and careful thinking
    form guidelines for a growing faith.

We believe we are starting here,
    in loving ways and obedient service,
    work worth finishing in heaven.

We believe we are being saved
    by the grace of God.
    Shout "Hallelujah!" and "Amen!"

BENEDICTIONS

1

This service is over, but our life in Jesus Christ goes on and on. If we live, we live for the Lord; if we die, we die in the Lord. Whether we live or die, we are the Lord's. Go live joyfully, as people who are safe both now and forever. Amen.

2

Grace and peace. May the blessing of God, whom we love as Father, Son, and Holy Spirit, be yours now and forever. Amen.

3

This time of worship is ended; now is the time for all good people to do the will of God. We are not our own; we have been bought with a price. So live for the Lord, live well and joyfully! Amen.

4

Now we go from the safety of this sanctuary into the human struggles of everyday life. God, please go before us to prepare the way for us to walk. In the name and Spirit of Jesus Christ our Lord. Amen.

5

As we have worshiped, we have been profoundly conscious of the presence and power of God. He does not let us down when we leave here; he always surrounds and supports us with his love. Go now to live in the name of the Father, Son, and Holy Spirit. Amen.

6

May God bless you and keep you safe, now and forever. Amen.

7

You are the light of the world. Let your light so shine that all who see you will come to worship God. Amen.

8

You are the salt of the earth. Go season all of life with the love of God and the power of the Holy Spirit, in the name of Jesus. Amen.

9

You are the leaven in the loaf. Go work the miracle of God's love at your job, in your neighborhood, in your family, until all are saved by the Power at work in you. Amen.

10

Move from worship into the world, counting upon God's gracious mercy and love. May the blessing of God Almighty, Father, Son, and Holy Spirit, be yours now and forever. Amen.

11

May God fill you with joy and peace. Live by the power of the Holy Spirit, in the name of Jesus Christ. Amen.

12

May all that we do be to the glory of God our Father and the Lord Jesus Christ, by the power of the Holy Spirit in us. Amen.

13

Who knows what new things may happen in the days ahead? Go in peace and love, secure in knowing that God watches over you and that your life is safe, now and forever. Amen.

BENEDICTIONS

14

God loves us with a steadfast love, no matter what we do. But should we continue to live in sin so that God's grace may abound? Of course not! Go live your faith, set free from sin by the Lord Jesus Christ! Amen.

15

Press on toward the mark of your high calling in Jesus Christ. Forget what lies behind; move on to make him your very own. Amen.

16

You are set free, now, to think and feel and do your very best for God, through our Lord Jesus Christ and by the power of the Holy Spirit. Amen.

17

To God be the glory, both now and forever! Go live as his people. Amen.

18

Go out now, to live in the world what we believe in our hearts and proclaim with our lips. Jesus Christ is Lord! Amen.

19

Nothing can separate us from the love of God. Wherever we go, or whatever we do, or whatever befalls us, the Eternal God is our refuge, and underneath are his everlasting arms. Amen.

20

Live as disciples of Jesus. Love one another as he loves you. Forgive, in his Spirit. Hope and rejoice in the Lord! The gospel is just that simple, because it is meant to be done. Amen.

21

Nothing can ever be the same, once we have heard the Word of God. Let us return to the scenes of our daily lives, expecting to see God at work, and ready to be led by his Holy Spirit. In the name of Christ. Amen.

22

Go now to do the will of God as you understand it, secure in knowing that God perfects all our work, in the power of the Holy Spirit, to the glory of Christ. Amen.

23

Go share your faith with someone who needs love, forgiveness, or hope. Point them toward God. Let him save them, as he is saving you. In the name of the Father, Son, and Holy Spirit. Amen.

24

Truly God's steadfast love is beyond our understanding. All our past is prologue to the great future God has for all of us. Go in peace and love, in the name of the Father, Son, and Holy Spirit. Amen.

25

God bless you. Christ love you. The Holy Spirit fill you. Amen.

26

Worship is only a preparation for living the Good News. Go now, to live toward others the gospel-according-to-you. In the name and Spirit of Jesus Christ our Lord. Amen.

27

To every time there is purpose, and reason for our being under heaven. What time is it? A time to love. A time to forgive one another. A time to mourn. A time to celebrate. Thanks be to God! All our times are in his hands. Amen.

28

Go live as people of God, in the name of Jesus and by the power of his Holy Spirit. Amen.

29

Look around you, at one another. See, God has given us each other to love. Others will know we are Christians by our love, too. Go live in the name of our Father, Son, and Holy Spirit. Amen.

30

May the peace that passes understanding fill your hearts. May the peace that the world cannot give or take away fill your minds. For you go out to live in the name of God, Father, Son, and Holy Spirit. Amen.

31

"Sin must not rule over you; you do not live under law but under God's grace." Thanks be to God! You can go now to live as people set free from the bondage of sin by Jesus Christ our Lord. Amen. [text from Romans 6:14 TEV]

32

"May God our Father and the Lord Jesus Christ give you grace and peace." Amen. [text from Philippians 1:2 TEV]

SERVICES OF
BAPTISM 〰〰〰〰〰〰〰〰

1
A SERVICE OF BAPTISM IN
MODERN ENGLISH

Today we celebrate the sacrament of baptism for *(child's name)*, as *(his, her)* parents introduce *(him, her)* into the whole family of God. Baptism is a sign of the grace of our Lord, and clearly tells us that *(child's name)* is now a part of the fellowship of the community of faith.

You may remember that Jesus' parents brought him to the Temple eight days after birth, to dedicate his life to God. Jesus himself, as a grown man, experienced baptism in the Jordan River at the hands of John. And Jesus himself said of children, "Do not stop the children. God's Kingdom is especially for them."

We invite the parents, family and sponsors to come now with *(child's name)*.

● *Here let the pastor offer the right hand of fellowship to those who have come to the front. If there are too many, offer the gesture at least to the parents.*

Will you, as *(his, her)* parents, speak for your child? Will you share with us your faith?
Yes. We will.
As you bring *(child's name)* for baptism, do you confess

your faith in Jesus Christ as your Lord and Savior?
Yes. We do.
As an act of faith, will you live a wholesome Christian
life, so that *(child's name)* will know *(he, she)* is part of a
Christian home?
Yes. We will.
When *(he, she)* is old enough to understand baptism,
will you explain to *(child's name)* what happened today?
Yes. We will.
(Child's name) is a part of this congregation and will be
entered on the Preparatory Roll until *(his, her)* full
confirmation in the church. Will you do all in your
power to keep *(child's name)* active in the church and in
Christian service? By your own participation, will you
encourage *(him, her)* in the life of faith?
Yes. We will.

● *The pastor will take the child to the bowl or font and
shall baptize the child, saying*
(Child's name), I baptize you in the name of the Father,
and the Son, and the Holy Spirit. Amen.

● *The pastor shall deliver the child to his or her parents and
ask the whole congregation to stand as the parents face
them.*

I commend to your loving care *(child's name)* and *(his,
her)* family. Live a wholesome Christian life, so *(child's
name)* will know intuitively what it means to follow
Christ. As a congregation, we will join together all our
resources to nurture this family in the life of Christ. As
we grow, they will grow as well. And God's Kingdom
will be more nearly complete. Will you do this?

CELEBRATIONS FOR TODAY

With God's help, we will do our best to follow Jesus Christ. We will try, honestly, to be a Christian influence in the life of (*child's name*) **and** (*his, her*) **family.**

Let us pray. Lord, we have acted in good faith this day. We offer to you not only this child, but ourselves. We offer you our hopes and longings for (*child's name*) to grow in wisdom, and in stature, and in favor with God and mankind. We ask your help in living a life consistent with the example of your Son, Jesus Christ. As we surround (*child's name*) with our love, may your love support us and lead us in the abundant life. This we ask in the name of Jesus our Lord. Amen.

2

BRIEF ORDER FOR BAPTISM

Baptism is a celebration of God's love for this person and for all people. Before we ever learn to love, God first loves us. Long before we respond in faith, God claims us. In this spirit of faith, Joseph and Mary took Jesus to the temple for the anointing with oil, as a sign of God's love. Later, in a personal response to God's love, Jesus was baptized by John with water. Whether we come to receive baptism as infants, as youth, or as adults, the meaning is the same. God loves us, and we are learning to love God in return. Baptism is a celebration of that relationship we call Christian faith.

Please come forward in faith, now, to celebrate together the sacrament of Holy Baptism. We invite family members and friends who are here to come forward as well.

(Child's, youth's, or adult's name), I baptize you in the name of the Father, Son, and Holy Spirit. Amen.

Let us pray. O God, we celebrate today your love for this person. May *(he, she)* grow in love and grace all the days of *(his, her)* life. As a community of faith, we surround *(him, her)* with our love. Help us witness to the way of Christ that leads to life eternal. Through the power of the Holy Spirit. Amen.

Go in peace, and may God's peace go with you. Amen.
3
AN EMERGENCY BAPTISMAL RITE
In this difficult situation, in this strange setting, you are still surrounded by the loving care of God. The God whom we know as Father, Son, and Holy Spirit would claim you as his own, now and forever. So we, here, celebrate his love with you.

(Child's, youth's, or adult's name), I baptize you in the name of the Father, Son, and Holy Spirit. Amen.

Almighty God our Father, you have made us for yourself. We are yours, now and forever, through Jesus Christ, by the Spirit at work in us. Amen.

COMMUNION RESOURCES

COMMUNION CALLS TO WORSHIP
1
Minister: Seek the Lord where he is to be found.
People: Call upon him while he is near.
Minister: God is great, and God is good.
People: Let us thank him for this food.
Minister: May God touch your life intimately.
People: And yours, as well. Amen.
2
Minister: Blessed are the poor,
People: For they have the Spirit.
Minister: Blessed are those who hunger,
People: For this bread and drink feed their souls.
Minister: Blessed are all people,
People: When we serve the Lord with gladness. Amen.
3
Minister: Jesus said, "This is my body, given for you."
People: Through this meal, we become one body.
Minister: Jesus said, "This cup is the new covenant."
People: Through our sharing, we become one in faith.

COMMUNION RESOURCES

Minister: Jesus said, "Prepare supper for me; gird yourself and serve me."

People: By serving him, we become his Church.

4

Minister: We are what we eat, in more ways than we imagine.

People: Come, let us feast of Christ so he may live again in us.

All: Amen.

5

Minister: The Peace of God: is it not for the whole human family?

People: Yes, we are one Word, one loaf, one cup, one world.

Minister: The Love of God: is it not for all people to share?

People: God's love is for everyone! We are one Word, one loaf, one cup, one world.

Minister: God has promised: "Behold, I make all things new."

People: Behold, we are one Word, one loaf, one cup, one world.

6

Out of all the times and places of our lives, we come to this sacred time and place for the one meal we all celebrate together. It is the Lord's Supper that we are about. Let no one hold back, out of fear or guilt. Here is love offered to you. Here is forgiveness for everything. Come let us prepare to feast!

7

We are the body of Christ, and members one of another. It is the mystery of ourselves that is laid upon the altar. It is the mystery of ourselves that we receive. It is to what we are, that we say Amen. [adapted from St. Augustine's *Confessions*]

8

We eat together with people we love. Behold the love of Christ in preparing and eating this meal together! He comes to us and lives in us. We can never be the same again.

9

Minister: The bread represents the body of Christ.

People: The cup represents his blood shed for us.

Minister: Let us celebrate the life of the risen Lord,

People: Which is beyond eating or drinking, but becomes part of our life together in him.

INVITATIONS TO COMMUNION

1

This is the table of the Lord. It is set in love. It is spread before us with compassion. It is to be consumed in faith. Come, now. Share in the feast of the Lord.

2

God's meal is open to you. He only asks that we come with honesty, share with him what we can, and leave intending to lead a better life. His meal is a source of spiritual strength for us all. Let us share it joyfully.

3

You are invited to share in this feast prepared to celebrate God's abundant love. Do you feel an urgency to improve your living? Do you sense an imperative to follow Jesus Christ? Do you have an awareness of the love your neighbor needs? Come join in this feast, for strength, courage, and love.

4

Would you like to be forgiven of your sins? Would you like to walk in love with your neighbors? Would you like to have the strength to lead a new life, patterned after Jesus Christ? You are invited to draw near with faith and to receive strength from his food.

5

Each person here is welcome at this meal of God's. It is freely given for our spiritual nourishment. If your intentions are to lead a new life in Christ, you are welcome. If your heart is willing to venture ordinary love with average people, you are welcome. If you are a part of this or any other household of faith, your faith in Jesus makes you welcome here.

6

Friends, if you sincerely turn your back on your sins; if you want to live in love and peace with everyone; if you desire to lead a new life doing God's will; then prepare to come forward in faith to receive this sacrament.

7

Are you ready for communion? Have you done your best to repent of your sins? Do you want to live as a neighbor to everyone? Will you try to do God's will, starting now? Then you have prepared the best you can. Trust God to complete the preparations for communion that we are making together.

8

We celebrate "open" communion. Anyone who wishes to commune may come. You do not have to be sinless; he forgives sin. You do not have to be good; he is perfecting us all. You need not belong to this or any church; he calls all people to this meal. It is enough, if you want to love the Lord and to follow him with all your heart. Come in faith. See what the Lord God offers you here. Go out to live, and never be the same again. This is all we ask. So come.

9

Come to this meal in memory of his life, death and resurrection. Come to this meal in the faith that he is risen and is here waiting. Come to this meal in the hope that we will be with him, forever. Come to this meal.

10

Communion has many meanings, personal and theological. But it is based on a simple human reality: we eat with those we love and avoid eating with those we cannot love. The message, then, is clear. God loves you enough to be with you in this meal. Feast upon his love.

ACTS OF CONSECRATION AND REMEMBRANCE

1

Minister:	This is the bread for our sharing in the Lord's meal.
People:	We will accept it thankfully!
All:	Father, we will begin, this day, to live a life that shows how Christ is alive inside. We shall put away all signs of weakness, through the sharing of this bread. We will unselfishly share our energies and abilities. May your Kingdom become more real to us, in the breaking of this bread.
Minister:	This is the cup for our sharing at God's table.
People:	We will accept it with joy!

COMMUNION RESOURCES

All: Lord, we will begin, this day, to live by the strength of your Word. We shall not count on our own strength. We shall not boast of our own power. As we share this cup of faith, we give ourselves to you. Lead us into life eternal. Amen.

2

Minister: Let those who would bring the bread to the table, for our congregation, come now.

Bread-bearer: We bring this loaf as a symbol of Christ's sacrifice and love for us all.

All: Bread of the world in mercy broken, wine of the soul in mercy shed, by whom the words of life were spoken, and in whose death our sins are dead.

Minister: Let those who would bring the cup to the table for our congregation, come now.

Cup-bearer: We bring this cup as a symbol of our salvation, in his death-for-us-all.

All: Look on the heart by sorrow broken. Look on the tears, by sinners shed. And be thy feast to us the token that by thy grace our souls are fed.

[text for the congregation is from the hymn "Bread of the World," which could be sung]

3

Minister: Jesus took the bread, and gave thanks, and broke it, and passed it to his friends.

People: His bread is life to us.

Minister: Jesus took the cup, and gave thanks, and passed it to his followers.

People: His cup is strength to us.

(continued)

All: O Lord, on the night you were betrayed, you were the servant. As we share this bread, we break open our lives to serve the world. After that supper, you poured out your life for all. As we share this cup, we give ourselves to you again. Use us in your paths of peace. Move us in your ways of love. Lead us in your work of faith. We are yours. Amen.

4

Almighty God, our Father: you gave your only Son for our redemption, in the suffering of the cross. We remember that sacrifice of love, with thanksgiving, as we celebrate this feast of faith. When we break the bread and pass the cup, we dedicate our lives to him who willingly chose the cross.

Lord Jesus, you gathered your disciples and washed their feet. You were betrayed by a dear friend. You were deserted by those who were closest to you. Forgive us when we betray you. Reconcile us when we desert you.

Holy Spirit of God, we pray for the strength to live the promises that we make in this feast. We ask for guidance: lead us to leave the table and to move into service. We need your power, as we try to follow the way of Jesus Christ. Grateful for this time, we need you in every time of life. Amen.

5

Almighty God, our heavenly Father, you gave Jesus to die on the cross for our salvation. Now freely give us all things. Fill us with your Holy Spirit, as we receive these elements of communion. They are, for us, symbols of the life of Jesus Christ. So we continue the celebration

74

of that life, remembering his death and believing his resurrection, until he comes again in glory.

We shall never forget that on the night he was betrayed, he took bread left over from the meal, and his own cup of wine, and shared them as his body and blood would soon be shared with the whole world. Then he and his disciples left the safety of the upper room, to put themselves in harm's way, for the salvation of the world.

Help us give our lives, even at risk of death, in order that others may come to love you God, as Father, Son, and Holy Spirit. Amen.

WORDS OF SHARING
1

This loaf and this cup represent the life of Christ offered to you. Eat and drink, remembering Christ died for you. Feed on him in your heart by faith, with thanksgiving and joy!

2

Here are symbols of the life of Christ, offered to you. Share them with love, and live together in Christ until he lives fully in you. Then his joy will be in you, and your enjoyment of life eternal will be complete!

DISMISSAL SENTENCES
1

"You are the light of the world." Let your light shine among others. Arise and spread the light of Christ's love, wherever you go. [text from Matthew 5:14]

2

"You are the salt of the earth." If the salt has lost its flavor it is useless. Arise and go to share the spice of new life with those you meet. [text from Matthew 5:13]

3

"Love one another. As I have loved you, so you must love one another." Arise and go, as instruments of his love. [text from John 13:34 TEV]

4

"You must be wise as serpents and as peaceful as doves." Arise and go into a complicated world, with the complete love of Christ. [text paraphrased from Matthew 10:16]

5

"You are not far from the kingdom of God." Arise and go joyfully. God is with you. [text from Mark 12:34]

6

Whoever is first shall be last; and whoever is last shall be first in the Kingdom. Arise and go, trust in God to provide a place for you.

7

"I am the vine, you are the branches." Stay rooted in him and you will live. Arise and go. God is with you. [text from John 15:5]

8

"Love your neighbor as yourself." You are loved by God, so you can love yourself and your neighbor. Be reconciled with one another, in the name of Jesus Christ. [text from Mark 12:31]

9

"Love the Lord your God with all your heart, soul, strength, and mind." His food has made you more loving. Go in peace. [text paraphrased from Mark 12:30]

10

Jesus said, "I came that all may have abundant life." Arise to go in peace, knowing that your abundant life in

Christ shall overflow with love and mercy. [text paraphrased from John 10:10]

11

Jesus said, "Go bear fruit, and your fruit shall abide." By the fruits of your life may all know you are loving followers of Jesus Christ our Lord. [text paraphrased from John 15:16]

12

Jesus said, "I am the bread of life. Those who come to me shall not hunger or thirst." Here, your hungering and thirsting after righteousness has been satisfied. Arise to go in peace. [text paraphrased from John 6:35]

13

Jesus said, "I am the way, and the truth, and the life." Christ shall lead you to truth and to life eternal, as you follow his way. Arise to go. [text from John 14:6]

14

Jesus said, "I am the door." May all your coming and going be a witness that you live in Christ and he lives in you. Go through the doors he opens and live forever. Arise to go in peace. [text from John 10:9]

15

Jesus said, "Whoever would save his life will lose it, and whoever loses his life for my sake will find it." By losing yourself in him, may you discover God's free gift of eternal life. Arise to go in peace. [text from Matthew 16:25]

16

Jesus said, "Let the one without sin cast the first stone. . . . What! Do none condemn you? Neither do I: go to sin no more." Arise to go. [text paraphrased from John 8:7-11]

17

Give to the poor, . . . and come follow me," Jesus said. Arise to be a neighbor to someone who needs your loving care. [text from Mark 10:21]

18

Jesus said, "Blessed are the poor in spirit, for theirs is the kingdom of heaven." In this simple act of faith we call communion, may Christ richly bless your life. Arise to go in peace. [text from Matthew 5:3]

19

Jesus said, "Blessed are those who mourn, for they shall be comforted." Arise to go, leaving with God all the sorrow your hearts may feel. You shall be comforted by the presence of the Holy Spirit. [text from Matthew 5:4]

20

Jesus said, "Blessed are the meek, for they shall inherit the earth." What does the Lord require of you, but to do justice, to love steadfastly, and to walk humbly with God? Arise to go and live forever. [text from Matthew 5:5]

21

Jesus said, "Blessed are those who hunger and thirst for righteousness, for they shall be satisfied." God, in his mercy, satisfies all the thirsts and hungers of our human hearts. Arise to go in peace. [text from Matthew 5:6]

22

Jesus said, "Blessed are the merciful, for they shall obtain mercy." You have celebrated the steadfast love of God here; now arise to go share it with others. [text from Matthew 5:7]

23

Jesus said, "Blessed are the peacemakers, for they shall be called sons and daughters of God." Make the peace of God central in your life, wherever you may find yourself surrounded by human conflict. Arise to go in peace. [text paraphrased from Matthew 5:9]

24

"Blessed are the pure in heart, for they shall see God," Jesus said. Purity of heart is to will one thing. Long for God, until all your spiritual struggles shall cease. Arise to go in peace. [text from Matthew 5:8]

25

Jesus said, "Blessed are those who are persecuted for righteousness' sake." Try to witness to and to minister to others, in the name of our Lord Jesus Christ. Risk misunderstanding and persecution. Arise to go in peace. [text from Matthew 5:10]

OTHER COMMUNION PRAYERS

1

O God our Father, before you our whole lives are exposed, and all our needs are known. Be at work in our lives. Wipe out all our old secrets and wrong desires, so that we may perfectly love you and truly worship you, in Jesus Christ our Lord. Amen.

2

We do not come to this table, O Lord, counting on our own goodness. For we know that we have missed the mark of our high calling. We trust only in your love. We would gladly eat the leftovers from your table. But we rejoice that your love is so great that you invite us to come as guests. Grant that we may receive this sacrament as a turning point in our lives. May we grow to be like you, as you become the center of our living. Amen.

3

O Lord our Father, please accept our offering of praise and thanksgiving. We thank you that in Jesus Christ we find forgiveness for all that is past and a new future of meaning and purpose.

Here and now, Lord, we offer our selves to you. We are yours, body and soul. May we all find our lives filled with grace and goodness. Though none of us deserve it, lead us to a new life together. In Jesus Christ our Lord. Amen.

MEMBERSHIP CELEBRATIONS

1
A CONFIRMATION CELEBRATION
The Church is a gift of God's for our spiritual nourishment and growth, and for service in the ministry of Jesus Christ. In the Church, we find comfort in its sacraments, warmth in its fellowship, nurture in its programs for learning, and opportunities for service in its other ministries. The Church is God's instrument of grace and discipleship, designed to free us from the power of temptation and to encourage us to serve and save the world.

● *Invite the confirmands to come forward, as previously rehearsed.*

I present these persons to you. They have come forward to be confirmed as full and responsible members of *(name of the church)*. Their confirmation is only one event in a lifelong process of learning and growing, as they become full disciples of the Lord Jesus Christ.

Do you here, in the presence of your friends and your families, affirm that you have received the sacrament of Christian baptism?
Yes. I do.

Do you accept Jesus Christ as your Savior and intend to follow him all your life?
With God's help, I will follow Christ.
Do you find God's Word in the Holy Bible; and are you willing to grow as you live its teachings in your life?
Yes. God's Word is alive in me.
Will you strive to be a follower of Jesus Christ, through the ministries and mission of the Church?
With God's help, I will live as the Church.
Do you want to be a part of this congregation of the Body of Christ?
Yes. I do.

● *All who are to be confirmed will kneel. The minister shall place his hand on the head of each confirmand in turn, with the following words.*

May the Lord strengthen and confirm you as a full member of the Church. May his Spirit lead you. May his peace be yours. Amen.

● *All present will rise to join in this or another appropriate act of affirming our Christian faith.*

I believe in God as Creator and Ruler of all things.
I believe in Jesus Christ as God's Son and my Savior.
I believe in the Spirit as God's presence to lead and direct my life.
I believe in the Church as the imperfect instrument of God, whose holy traditions, sacraments, preaching, and services witness to God in the world.
I believe in the final triumph of good over evil, and of life over death.

I believe in the Resurrection as God's loving promise to those who are faithful.
I believe, as God leads me, I will live forever. Amen.

2

A RECEPTION OF MEMBERS BY
PROFESSION OF FAITH

Explanation   Minister

When we join any local church that worships God as Father, Son, and Holy Spirit, we are joining ourselves to the whole Christian Church. On behalf, then, of the worldwide fellowship of Christians, we welcome into membership today *(announce the full name and greet each person in turn). (These people, this person) (have, has)* been baptized, *(have, has)* been instructed and counseled in the meaning of church membership, and *(are, is)* now ready to celebrate the calling to be the Church in the world.

Questions to Those Being Received   Minister

Do you believe, as your baptism signified, that God loves you and claims you as one of his people?
I do.

Do you accept Jesus Christ as your Lord and Savior, and will you follow him as a faithful disciple all your life?
I do, and I will.

Will you live by your understanding of the Christian faith as interpreted from the scriptures of the Holy Bible?
I will.

Do you promise, by God's grace, to live a Christian life and to be the Church in the world?
I do.

Will you be loyal to this congregation, so long as you can share in its life? Then will you transfer to other local congregations of the Christian Church, wherever you may move?

I will.

● *All kneel, for the pastor to lay his hand upon their heads in turn.*

Laying on of Hands   Minister

(Full name of the person), the Lord God defend you with his heavenly grace. May the Holy Spirit confirm you in the faith and fellowship of all true disciples of Jesus Christ. Amen.

Instructions   Minister

We believe it is the duty and privilege of every Christian to be active in some local congregation. We are all called into some local community of love and service. You are now a member of this church and of the worldwide Christian community. Uphold some local fellowship, wherever you may live, with your prayers, your presence, your gifts and your service.

Welcome by the Congregation   All

We welcome you into membership in Christ's holy Church. We celebrate your joining this congregation, for your faith completes our joy. Be the Church with us, gathered for study and worship, scattered for living service to others. In the name of the Father, Son, and Holy Spirit. Amen.

Dismissal *(optional)*   Minister

Go in peace. Be of good courage. Love what is good. Hate all evil. May the blessing of God be with you and remain with you forever. Amen.

3

ORDER FOR RECEIVING MEMBERS
BY TRANSFER

Introduction   Minister

Recognizing that this congregation is part of a worldwide community of Christians, we welcome into membership in our church *(this person, these persons)* who *(is, are)* transferring *(his, her, their)* membership. *(Announce the full name of each person transferring, and announce the names of any children being added to the Preparatory Membership Roll.)*

Minister's Welcome   Minister

We welcome *(the person's or family's name)*, coming from *(local church's name)* in *(locality)*.

Welcome by the Congregation   All

You have been a member of the Christian community elsewhere, and we rejoice in welcoming you to this congregation. Be the Church with us, as we gather for study and worship, and then scatter for living service to others. In the name of the Father, Son, and Holy Spirit. Amen.

Instructions   Minister

We expect you to support this local church with your prayers, your presence, your gifts, and your service. We will join you in prayer, in worship and study, in giving to God's work, and in serving others.

Prayer   Minister

Lord, you call us out of our separate lives to be your Church. Send your Spirit upon us, so that we may press on toward the mark of our high calling. Amen.

WEDDING
CELEBRATIONS

1

A MARRIAGE CELEBRATION

Explanation   Minister

We are together today, in the presence of God and of our families and friends, to celebrate the union of *(groom's full name)* and *(bride's full name)* in marriage. We believe God blesses the bonds of a marriage, even as Jesus blessed the wedding in Cana of Galilee with his first public miracle. Marriage is a serious relationship for *(groom's first name)* and *(bride's first name)* to form, in full partnership with God.

Opportunity to Stop the Service *(optional)*   Minister

If any person can show just cause why these two should not be lawfully joined, let him or her speak now.

Reminder to the Couple   Minister

I am going to ask you both to answer certain historic questions to indicate your readiness to enter the covenant of marriage. I will help you express your promises to each other, to love each other in Christ's name. As you speak these most important words to each other, we all are listening and supporting you with our love, hope, and joy. God blesses those who love in his way and obey his will with a wholesome, fulfilling life together.

Questions to the Couple   Minister

(Groom's first name), will you enter into marriage with

this woman? Will you love, respect, and support her through good times and bad?

I will.

(Bride's first name), will you enter into marriage with this man? Will you love, respect, and support him through good times and bad?

I will.

Giving Away the Bride *(optional)*   Minister

Today these two persons are slackening their familiar bonds with parents to enter a new relationship with each other that will create a new family, a new home. It is appropriate that their parents bless their union. Who gives this woman into marriage as a blessing of her continuing maturity?

I do *or* **We do.**

(Optional: Who gives this man into marriage as a blessing of his continuing maturity?)

Joining their Hands   Minister

The minister shall receive the couple's right hands into his as they face each other to speak their own promises to each other. If they wish, he may help them recite their promises, by acting as prompter.

The Promises   Couple

I, *(groom's first name),* accept you as my wife, to respect and to love, today and beyond, for better and for worse, in sickness and in health, for richer or poorer. And, as it is God's will, I pledge myself to you.

I, *(bride's first name),* accept you as my husband, to respect and to love, today and beyond, for better and for worse, in sickness and in health, for richer or poorer. And, as it is God's will, I pledge myself to you.

87

Exchange of Rings *(optional)*   Minister

The wedding ring is a visible sign of the marriage of *(groom's first name)* and *(bride's first name)*. It is a circle without end, symbolizing the unending presence of God in this covenant. Let us pray.

Bless, O Lord, the giving and receiving of *(this, these)* ring*(s)* as a sign of love, peace, and hope. Be with this couple in the times ahead. Amen.

Wedding Vows   Couple

As he places the ring on her finger:

This is a sign of my love for you. With this ring, I seal our marriage, in the name of the Father, Son, and Holy Spirit. Amen.

As she places the ring on his finger:

This is a sign of my love for you. With this ring, I seal our marriage, in the name of the Father, Son, and Holy Spirit. Amen.

Announcement of Wedding   Minister

(Groom's first name) and *(bride's first name)* are just beginning to celebrate their marriage. May they continue to enjoy each other as long as they live. We have heard their promises, witnessed their sharing of rings, and shared their joy. With great pleasure, I tell you all that *(groom's first name)* and *(bride's first name)* are husband and wife together, in the name of the Father, Son, and Holy Spirit. Amen.

Pastoral Prayer for the Couple

(as they kneel)   Minister

O Lord God, we rejoice in your presence in this holy celebration of marriage. Be with them, as they share the joys and struggles of a creative marriage. Give them a full measure of grace, so they may live in love and harmony, and grow in patience and enthusiasm.

May they live here, and forever, as part of your Kingdom. Amen.

Benediction *(all standing)*   Minister

The Lord bless you. The Lord shine upon you. The Lord be gracious to you, and give you his peace. Amen.

N.B. These words of liturgy may be surrounded by or combined with other acts of celebration and music, as appropriate.

2

A WEDDING SERVICE IN MODERN ENGLISH

Opening Words   Minister

We are gathered together here in the sight of God, and in the presence of these witnesses, to join together *(groom's full name)* and *(bride's full name)* in holy matrimony. Into this holy estate they have come now to be joined. If anyone can show serious cause why they may not be wed, let him now speak, or keep silent forever.

Giving of the Bride   Whoever Is Designated

Who gives this woman to be married to this man?

I do *or* **We do** *or* **Her mother and I do,** *etc.*

(The one giving the bride away resumes his seat in the congregation.)

Statement to the Couple   Minister

I remind you both, as you stand in the presence of God, that these vows you are about to make are serious. You are about to declare before your families and friends your faithful pledge to each other. Be assured that if you keep your solemn vows, and if you try to do God's will toward each other, God will bless your marriage, will grant you fulfillment in it, and will keep your home in peace.

Question to the Groom   Minister

(Groom's first name), are you willing to take *(bride's full name)* to be your wife, to live together in marriage? Will you love her, comfort her, honor and support her, in sickness and in health? Will you devote yourself to her as long as you both may live?

Yes, I am willing.

Question to the Bride   Minister

(Bride's first name), are you willing to take *(groom's full name)* to be your husband, to live together in marriage? Will you love him, comfort him, honor and support him, in sickness and in health? Will you devote yourself to him as long as you both may live.

Yes, I am willing.

(The bride may hand her bouquet to her bridesmaid, to free her hands. Then the minister shall ask the couple to join hands and face each other to repeat [after him] their vows to each other.)

The Groom's Vow   Groom

I, *(groom's first name)*, take you *(bride's first name)*, to be my wife, to love and to cherish, from this day forward, for better or for worse, for richer or for poorer, in sickness and in health, so long as we shall live. This pledge I make to you in good faith.

The Bride's Vow   Bride

I, *(bride's first name)*, take you *(groom's first name)*, to be my husband, to love and to cherish, from this day forward, for better for for worse, for richer or for poorer, in sickness and in health, so long as we shall live. This pledge I make to you in good faith.

Explanation of the Ring(s)   Minister

(This ring, these rings) (is, are) to be a visible sign to all people of the unending love that *(groom's first name)* and *(bride's first name)* pledge to each other in their Christian marriage.

Giving of the Ring(s)   Couple

(Bride's first name/groom's first name), I give this ring to you as an expression of my constant faith and abiding love.

Announcement to the Congregation   Minister

(Groom's first name) and *(bride's first name)* have joined in marriage before God, in your presence today. They have pledged their lives to each other, by joining hands and by giving and receiving ring(s). I announce that they are husband and wife, in the name of all that is holy. Let no one or anything come between these two people who have joined their lives.

(Groom's first name) and *(bride's first name)* realize what solemn vows they have just made. As they begin their married life together, they invite your spoken or silent prayers. Now we will have a time for informal, spontaneous prayer together. If you wish to share out loud your prayer for them, please feel free to do that. Or you may pray in silence for them. When everyone who wishes has offered prayer, we will end with our modern English Lord's Prayer in the wedding bulletin. Let us pray.

(Here may follow a reasonable period of spoken or silent prayer.)

The Modern English Lord's Prayer   All

Our Father, may all people come to respect and to love you. May you rule in every person and in all of life. Give us, day by day, the things of life we need.

91

Forgive us our sins, for we forgive everyone who has done us wrong. Let nothing test us beyond our strength. Save us from our weakness. For yours is the authority, and the power, and the glory forever. Amen.

Dismissal Benediction   Minister

May God bless your life together. May he give you grace to love, honor, and cherish each other. May you live together in faithfulness, patience, wisdom, and joy, now and forever. Amen.

3

A MODERN ENGLISH CELEBRATION
OF MARRIAGE

To celebrate a common law or other relationship in which a man and a woman have been living together.

Prelude

During the prelude, the wedding party shall make all final preparations. Guests will be seated by ushers, so that all have good seats. When all is ready and the time has arrived, the bride's mother will be escorted to her place, as a signal for the prelude to conclude.

Solo *(optional)*

Processional

The groom, best man, and minister will enter from the side door, take their places, and watch the rest of the wedding party process, as is traditional. When all are in place and the processional is concluded, the minister will direct the congregation to be seated.

Word of Welcome   Minister

Welcome to the wedding of *(groom's full name)* and *(bride's full name)*. Marriage is a serious commitment for two people to make toward one another. *(Groom's first name)* and *(bride's first name)* have discovered such joy and fulfillment in their love for one another that they are ready to celebrate, in your presence, what has happened and is happening between them.

Giving of the Bride   Her Father or Someone Else
Who gives this woman to be married to this man?
I do *or* **We do** *or* **Her mother and I do.**
(He leaves to take his place in the congregation.)

Word With the Couple   Minister
Addressing the couple by their first names: You both understand and deeply feel the profound meaning marriage has for you. You have already started to join your lives in a growing relationship that will continue to mature in the years ahead.

You chose this unique kind of wedding service to express in your own way how very much you love each other, and how very much you want your families and friends to share in your wedding.

Only the greatest courage, based on your deep and abiding love, lets you join your two lives to share an unknown future. It is an act of deepest faith to wed each other for life, come what may.

Questions to the Couple   Minister
(Groom's first name), in your mind and heart, is this woman, *(bride's first name),* your wife?
Yes.
(Bride's first name), in your mind and heart, is this man, *(groom's first name),* your husband?
Yes.

Blessing by the Minister
May God bless your marriage, grant you fulfillment in it, and let your love be a source of joy and peace, now and forever. Amen.

CELEBRATIONS FOR TODAY

Exchange of Rings and Kisses

(The minister receives the rings, shows them to the congregation, and explains their purpose.)

(This ring, these rings) shall let everyone know that *(groom's first name)* and *(bride's first name)* are husband and wife. Let no one come between them.

(The groom places the ring on the third finger of the bride's left hand and then may kiss her. The bride places the ring on the third finger of the groom's left hand and then may kiss him.)

Announcement of Marriage   Minister

Since *(groom's first name)* and *(bride's first name)* have come together to be married;

Since in their minds and hearts, they consider themselves to be husband and wife;

Since they have held hands and exchanged rings and kisses as symbols of their love;

Since they intend, with all sincerity, to share the future together, whatever it may hold,

(groom's first name) and *(bride's first name)*, Mr. and Mrs. *(groom's full name)*, I pronounce you husband and wife. May God bless your marriage.

Prayer for the Married Couple   All

O God, bless *(groom's first name)* and *(bride's first name)*. We join with you in loving them and in wishing them well for all of life. As they live together, God, may they continue to find love, joy, and peace in their marriage. Amen.

The Kiss of Joy   Couple
Recessional Music   As All Recess
Ushering Family and Honored Guests   Ushers
Postlude

FUNERAL RESOURCES~~~~

1

A MODERN ENGLISH FUNERAL SERVICE
Adapted from the United Methodist tradition
Scripture Sentences   Minister
   The eternal God is your dwelling place, and under-
   neath are the everlasting arms. [Deuteronomy 33:27a]

   Blessed be the Lord!
      for he has heard the voice of my
         supplications.
   The Lord is my strength and my shield;
   in him my heart trusts. [Psalm 28:6]

   None of us lives for himself only, none of us dies for
   himself only; if we live, it is for the Lord that we live,
   and if we die, it is for the Lord that we die. Whether
   we live or die, then, we belong to the Lord. For Christ
   died and rose to life in order to be the Lord of the
   living and of the dead. [Romans 14:7-9 TEV]

   For we know that when this tent we live in—our
   body here on earth—is torn down, God will have a
   house in heaven for us to live in, a home he himself
   made, which will last for ever. [II Corinthians 5:1
   TEV]

CELEBRATIONS FOR TODAY

Hymn *(Optional, but where used, it should be a strong tune sung as an affirmation of faith, in celebration of our life before God.)*

Call to Prayer   Minister
God lets us live in our bodies as long as we possibly can. Then, when we can live here no more, he gives us a way to live forever. Faced with death, shocked by great loss, we may have difficulty knowing what to pray. But if we turn to the Lord, he is our comfort and our help. Let us join our hearts in this prayer.

Prayer for Comfort   By the Minister or by All
Almighty God, our Creator, you have given us life as a gift. We thank you now, for the gift of this person's life. We have loved *(him, her)* and enjoyed *(him, her)*. *(His, her)* death is a great loss to us. Even now, as we struggle to accept what has happened, we turn to you for all the comfort and help that you have promised. Even 'as we grieve, we trust your goodness and mercy.

O Jesus, our Savior, you have conquered death in a wonderful way. Prepare a place for this loved one, and receive *(him, her)* to be where you are. We cannot imagine what eternal life beyond death is like, but we trust in you. May our spirits grow calm and our hearts be comforted, as we receive your assurance that *(he, she)* is safe forever.

O Holy Spirit, fill us with power, even as we feel our helplessness. Grant us the peace of God that passes understanding, even as our hearts are troubled. Comfort us with your presence, now and forever. Always we end our prayer as Jesus taught us.

The Lord's Prayer   In Unison

Words from the Word   The Minister or Friends
All our times are in God's hands. He will lead us through this experience of sorrow together. In the Psalms, we can take comfort in these words of testimony.

(Read Psalm 23, 27, 90, or 121; or any two of them.)

It is our faith in Christ that gives us strength and courage to face death not as the end, but as a beginning. As Jesus faced his own death, he prepared his own disciples. What he taught them can speak to us, too.

(Read John 14:1-7, 15-17, 27 from TEV or some other modern version.)

The apostle Paul witnesses to the great hope that we have in Jesus Christ our Lord.

(Read excerpts from Romans 8:14ff. or I Corinthians 15:20ff.)

Our hope in Jesus will not fail us. The time John envisioned in his book of Revelation is coming.

(Read Revelation 21:2-7 from TEV or another modern version.)

What else can we say? Who or what can separate us from the love of Christ? Nothing in all creation, not even death, shall be able to separate us from the love of God in Christ Jesus our Lord. And His Holy Spirit is our Comforter in this and every time.

Sermon or Eulogy *(optional, at specific request of family)*

Prayer for Inner Peace   Minister
O God, whom we know and love as Father, Son, and Holy Spirit:

Comfort and support us in our distress. Give us all the assurance that your people are precious, and do live forever with you. Your mercy endures forever. Grant us your peace. We thank you for this person, whom we have known and loved as best we could. Now we in faith entrust (his, her) life to you. In the name of the Father, Son, and Holy Spirit. Amen.

Passing the Peace (optional)   All

Let each of us turn to as many of those around us as we can to express God's love to each other and to support each other with signs of peace and affection. You may want to say "Peace," or "God be with you." Or you may want to say other words of support and comfort of your own. Or you may greeet one another with handshakes or hugs, as symbols of God's love. Care for each other, in your own way. When we are through, I will pronounce the benediction.

(Adequate time should be given; end when appropriate.)

Benediction   Minister

As you turn to God, may his peace be yours even in this sad time. Be in the world, as Jesus was. Forgive and love one another in his name. Let the risen Christ care for you. Welcome the Holy Spirit to be your Comforter. In the name of the Father, Son, and Holy Spirit. Amen.

At the place of committal, after all have gathered, this liturgy may be used.

Scriptural Affirmations   Minister

Our help is in the name of the Lord, who made heaven and earth. [Psalm 124:8]

As a father has compassion on his children, so the

98

Lord cares for those who love him. [paraphrase of Psalm 103:13]

Be strong. Fear not! Your God will come to save you. [paraphrase of Isaiah 35:4]

Act of Committal *(optional, at wish of family or minister involved)*

Words of Committal   Minister
Almighty God has already received the life of this person we love. *(He, she)* is already safe forever, with Jesus. May the Spirit of God continue to comfort us over our great loss, to the glory of God.
   We commit this body to the ground, looking for the resurrection and longing for life in the world to come. Blessed are all who rest in the Lord, now and forever. Through our Lord Jesus Christ. Amen.

Benediction   Minister
May the love of God, the grace of Jesus Christ, and the comfort of the Holy Spirit be yours. Amen.

Signs of Love and Care   The Minister and Others

N.B. Where hymnals or songbooks may not be available, as in a home or at a funeral establishment, words of any familiar hymn can be reproduced and distributed before the service begins. Prayers or other parts to be read, or even the entire service, may be reproduced as a bulletin.

2

ALTERNATE SCRIPTURES

Genesis 15:12-15   Isaiah 25:6-9

CELEBRATIONS FOR TODAY

Genesis 46:29-30
Genesis 48:10-11
Genesis 49:29-33
Deuteronomy 30:15-16, 19-20
Job 5:17-21, 24-25
Job 14:7-14
Ecclesiastes 3:1-9
Psalm 18:1-3, 24-25
Psalm 107:1-3, 33-43

Isaiah 65:17-25
Jeremiah 10:19-20, 23-24
Matthew 16:24-28
John 5:19-24
Romans 6:3-5
Romans 8:14-17
I Corinthians 15:12-22
II Corinthians 4:7-18
Others you may choose

Scriptural passages should be chosen with sensitivity to meet the emotional and spiritual needs of those who are mourning. The wise pastor listens to what people are feeling as they grieve; then he chooses from all the words of Scripture the Word that they may need to hear in that grief situation.

3

ALTERNATE AFFIRMATIONS AND ASSURANCES
Who has believed what we have heard? And to whom has the arm of the Lord been revealed? Surely he has borne our griefs and carried our sorrows. [Isaiah 53:1, 4a]

For the Lord will not cast off for ever, but, though he cause grief, he will have compassion according to the abundance of his steadfast love; for he does not willingly afflict or grieve the sons of men. [Lamentations 3:31-33]

Set me as a seal upon your heart, O Lord. For love is as strong as death. Many waters cannot quench love, nor floods drown it. [paraphrase of Song of Solomon 8:6a, 7]

100

Truly, truly, I say to you, you will weep and lament, but the world will rejoice; you will be sorrowful, but your sorrow will turn into joy. So you have sorrow now, but I will see you again and your hearts will rejoice, and no one will take your joy from you [John 16:20, 22]

I will not leave you desolate; I will come to you. Yet a little while, and the world will see me no more, but you will see me; because I live, you will live also [John 14:18-19]

4

ALTERNATE PRAYERS WITH THOSE WHO MOURN

Lord Jesus, you are our resurrection and our life. As we live, we live for you. If we die, we die in you. So whether we live or die, we are yours. Lord, give us in this time of sorrow a secure faith that our dear friend and loved one has not died eternally, but shall live forever with you.

All our times are in your hands. Comfort us as we genuinely mourn. Give us grace to worship you, and to receive your steadfast love, even as we face the reality of this death. May we put our whole trust in your goodness and mercy. Send your Spirit, now, to fill our lives so that our hearts may grow calm and our spirits recover. In the name of God, Father, Son, and Holy Spirit. Amen.

Almighty God, you are the source and ultimate destination of all our living. We dwell secure in your steadfast love, generation after generation. Provide refuge and strength in this time of trouble, so that we may walk and not faint, so that our spirits may mount up with wings like the eagles. Increase our faith, in this crisis, so we may know in our human experience of mourning the triumph over death that all have, who live forever in Christ Jesus our Lord. Amen.

We wait now, Lord, for you to grant us your comfort and your peace in this hour. We confess that we are slow to accept death as a part of your plan for life. We confess how reluctantly we surrender this friend and loved one into eternal care. You know the depth of our shock and sorrow, Jesus. You, too, wept beside a grave.

Let the Holy Spirit, your promised Comforter, come upon each of us now. Fill us with your love and inward peace, as we reach out to comfort one another. Be our companion as we live the sometimes painful days ahead. Even as we mourn, inspire all we feel, think, say, and do, to be a witness to our faith as Christians. Amen.

Jesus Christ, our risen Lord: you have gone before us into death, to prepare the way. Come again into our hearts and lives in this time of sorrow. Give us each our own experience of your love and of the comfort of your Spirit's presence. Thank you for preparing and giving a place, in the Kingdom of God, to this dear friend and loved one. Receive *(him, her)* unto yourself, that where you are *(he, she)* may be also. At *(his, her)* coming into the Kingdom, may there be great rejoicing and celebration, even as we mourn our loss. We confess that we are, even now, feeling deeply the pain of separation. Death is still a source of anxiety and fear to us, for we have not experienced it in our own bodies. Yet we count upon your having prepared a place for us and for all who love you. In the hours and days ahead, in all the times of our lives, come be with us to claim us as your own. Give us life eternal, beginning here and now. In the name of God, led by your Holy Spirit, we ask you these simple things. Amen.

Almighty God, we know not what to say or to pray in the face of such a tragic death. You know all that we are experiencing; come touch and minister to each of us in your way. Through Jesus Christ, Amen.

5
AN ALTERNATE COMMITTAL SERVICE

Scripture Selections
In thee, O Lord, do I seek refuge;
let me never be put to shame;
in thy righteousness deliver me!
Incline thy ear to me,
   rescue me speedily!
Be thou a rock of refuge for me,
   a strong fortress to save me!
. . . I trust in thee, O Lord,
   I say, "Thou art my God."
My times are in thy hand; . . .
Let thy face shine on thy servant.
                    [Psalm 31:1-2, 14-16a]

O how abundant is thy goodness,
   which thou hast laid up . . .
for those who take refuge in thee,
   in the sight of the sons of men! . . .
Blessed be the Lord,

for he has wondrously shown his
    steadfast love . . .

[Psalm 31:19, 21*a*]

Act of Committal

None of us lives to himself, and none of us dies to himself. If we live, we live for the Lord; and if we die, we die for the Lord. Whether we live or die—we are the Lord's! In our grief, we must entrust *(the person's full name)* to God at this time. *(He, She)* entered life as a miracle of God's love, and now has entered the everlasting miracle of his presence. Blessed are those who have fallen asleep in the Lord; may they rest from their labors, and may their works follow after them.

Let us pray:

Surely, O Lord, you understand our grief, and feel with us our sense of separation and sorrow. Visit us with your compassion and mercy. Look with tenderness and love upon this family and these friends, as they turn in faith and trust to you. Walk with us from this moment of sorrow, as we begin to turn again to our everyday lives. This we ask in the name of Jesus Christ, who is our resurrection and our life. Amen.

TABLE GRACES

1
For daily bread, for others fed,
We give you thanks, O Lord. Amen.

2
Grace our lives that they may be
Offerings of love to thee.
By thy hand we all are fed,
Thank thee, Lord, for daily bread. Amen.

3
By your Word our souls are led
To share with others daily bread.
Bring them to the gospel feast,
Rich and poor, great and least. Amen.

4
Make this meal a sacred time,
As I offer what is mine.
Make it yours, a holy feast,
Shared with all the last and least. Amen.

5
Make known to us in broken bread
Your Way, in which our lives are led.
Others, as well, would come to be
Guests at your table, all set free. Amen.

6
Bread of the world, for all of us broken,
Cup of the world, for all of us poured,

Help us to share this food as a token
Of your great love for all of the world. Amen.

7

God,
You know we are grateful
For every mouthful. Amen.

8

Grace our table with your presence,
And our lives with your love. Amen.

9

Eternal Father,
Thank you for this food and for your love. Amen.

10

Lord, how we love to laugh and be happy,
Trying our best to lead your new life.
Thanks for this food, as symbol of your love. Amen.

11

When we gather to eat, Lord,
It is always around your table.
Thanks for this food.
Help us to love each other with your love. Amen.

PRAYERS WITH
THE SICK ~~~~~~~~~~~~~~~~~~~~~

● Some of these prayers are appropriate for the sick person along with his or her family and friends; some are for the family of the sick person; others are for the individual suffering illness alone. Prayers for the sick person may be prayed by the minister on behalf of the person, using "I" and "me," etc. Or, the prayers may be spoken for the individual, using the person's name in place of pronouns.

1

O God, be with us all in this time of illness. Your presence alone can make the difference between disease and health. Comfort with your love. Heal by your power. Loosen the bonds that hold and set us free. In the name of Father, Son, and Holy Ghost. Amen.

2

O God, I may not be good company when I am ill. But I pray out of the bottom of my heart for your presence and power. May your love bring wholeness of life. Let the spirit grow calm, as your healing comes. Strengthen my loved ones and friends, as they, too, support me with their concern. Underneath are your everlasting arms, and I know my life is forever safe. In the name and Spirit of Jesus. Amen.

3

Lord, God, all our times are in your hands. In this hard time, strengthen the faith to endure and to have victory. If life continues, it is a life for you. If death comes, we trust in you. Whether we live or die, we are always yours, body and soul. We continue to love you, and to look to you for every need. Amen.

4

Jesus, we thank you for surrounding us with your healing love, and with the love of so many concerned friends. Now that the worst is behind, may recovery and return to daily life be soon accomplished. May life never be taken for granted. And may we rejoice every day for the opportunities we have to serve others. Amen.

5

Our Father God, we pray for your presence and your love. Amen.

6

God, the operation just ahead is frightening. You know our fear of suffering. You understand the anxieties the next few days will bring. Just as the cross was a grim prospect for our Lord Jesus, so this operation is an intimidating prospect. We turn to you in faith, hoping for the comforting power of the Holy Spirit. Let the heart grow calm, the mind rest easy, secure in your loving care. You watch over us, now and always. Amen.

7

Eternal God, we offer prayer for the doctors, nurses, and specialists to whom we trust our lives. Guide their thoughts and actions as they do their very best to restore health. Help us to accept their ministries, and to return their love with patience and endurance. Thank you for this place of rest, this community of healing. To all our human efforts, add your presence and power. In the name of Jesus. Amen.

8

Father, we do not know what to ask. We pray earnestly that healing may take place and life may return, because we love *(person's name)*. Yet, to prolong life at the cost of suffering is not loving. You know how confused and desperate we are. Come minister to us. Help us sort through all we are feeling, to discover your way in this situation. Resolve this crisis in your way, as we trust in you. Give us courage and wisdom in this and every time of need. Amen.

9

Lord, what can we say? We have poured out our hearts in conversation with each other, and in prayer to you. We are speechless and helpless, and can only wait for your Word to comfort and sustain us. Love us. Save us. In spite of all, we love you. Amen.

10

Father, God, help us. We need your presence and your love so much. We are tired; give us strength to endure. We are discouraged; give us hope to triumph over all. When the body becomes too great a burden to bear, set the spirit free in your way and in your time. Thanks for a life as long as *(person's name)*'s has been. Now bestow eternal life, and new beginnings, as you have promised us in Jesus our Lord. You know our every longing, our every feeling, our every need. Care for us, through your Holy Spirit. Amen.

11

Lord Jesus, death may be near. You know how it feels to face your own death. Be a companion in this desperate time. You showed the world triumph over the body, over the grave. Now we look forward to welcome into your Kingdom, to be with you forever. Take the little faith we have, and in return give us the great strength to face this time together. Surround us with loving care and claim us as your own. In the name of the Father, Son, and Holy Spirit. Amen.

12

Almighty God, into your keeping I commit my life. Human hands and hearts have done all they can. Now it is up to you. I pray for healing and for wholeness of life. You know my deepest longings for health; but whether I live or die, I am yours. You have made me for yourself. You have saved me in Jesus Christ. You have watched over me in life. Now rescue me from death. My faith may falter, but your love never fails. See me through this and every time. Amen.

13

God, we thank you our faith does not desert us, even when our bodies are taking us to death. Give *(person's name)* the victory through our Lord Jesus Christ. Send your Holy Spirit to lead *(him, her)* to life eternal. Amen.

14

Father, we're scared and anxious. This is one of the toughest times we have ever faced together. Draw us closer together, as we trust in your love. Only your love can overcome our fears. Strengthen and uphold each of us, until this crisis is past. Naturally, we pray for recovery and for health for *(person's name)*. But if the worst comes, help us to trust you still, and to return your love. See us through this and every time of life. Speak your "Peace, be still" to our very troubled lives. Amen.

15

Lord, I am going home from this hospital tomorrow. What a miracle that is! Thanks for all the people who have cared for me during this illness. Thanks for my recovery to full Christian life and service. Amen.

16

Father, how good it is to be home again. My own bed is a welcome change. The home-cooked food tastes better than ever. My family has received me with love I find nowhere else, except with you. Thank you. Let strength and healing continue to come as gifts from you. For when I am back to normal completely, then I will pick up my Christian life with joy and abandon. Again, thanks. Amen.

17

Almighty God, you know how hard it is to be shut in all day, every day. The world becomes a few rooms, and dependence upon others is a fact of life. In this and every time of life, Lord, make us yours. In Christ, forgive our sins. Through the Holy Spirit, send us your peace. Amen.